W9-BOA-275

REVOLUTIONS IN THE THIRD WORLD

INTERNATIONAL STUDIES
IN
SOCIOLOGY AND SOCIAL ANTHROPOLOGY

General Editor

K. ISHWARAN

VOLUME LIV

QUEE-YOUNG KIM

REVOLUTIONS IN THE THIRD WORLD

REVOLUTIONS IN THE THIRD WORLD

EDITED BY

QUEE-YOUNG KIM

E.J. BRILL
LEIDEN · NEW YORK · KØBENHAVN · KÖLN
1991

The paper in this book meets the guidelines for performance and durability of the Committee on Production Guidelines for Book Longevity of the Council on Library Resources.

Library of Congress Cataloging-in-Publication Data

Revolutions in the Third World / edited by Quee-Young Kim.
    p.   cm.—(International studies in sociology and social anthropology, ISSN 0074-8684; v. 54)
   Includes bibliographical references and index.
   ISBN 90-04-09355-9
   1. Revolutions—Developing countries. I. Kim, Quee-Young.
II. Series.
HM281.R485   1990
303.6'4'091724—dc20
                                        90-23514
                                        CIP

ISSN   0074-8684
ISBN   90 04 09355 9

PRINTED IN THE NETHERLANDS

CONTENTS

Introduction

Paradigms and Revolutions: The Societal and Statist Approaches Reconsidered

QUEE-YOUNG KIM*

ABSTRACT

Protests, strikes, coups d'etat, revolts, rebellions and revolutions occur often throughout much of the developing world. Theorists have offered explanations about the origins, processes and outcomes. The most recent and influential paradigm is the state-centered structural approach. I review historically the development of various paradigms, including the society-centered "societal" approach. There are some useful insights in these views that one can use in the analysis of revolutionary movements. However, there are several serious inadequacies. The essays in this collection raise a number of important issues and offer findings, insights and directions that should contribute to the development of an emerging paradigm that is based not just on the state but a dialectical society-state relationship.

PHILOSOPHERS, REVOLUTIONARIES and social scientists have all contributed to our knowledge of revolution. Philosophers interpreted what revolutionaries had done; social scientists built paradigms to understand and explain revolutions. The theoretical images of what revolution is and ought to do varied according to changes in philosopical focus and interest but the pattern of these images has been primarily shaped by three concomitant influences: the influence generated by the surrounding scene of real or imagined revolution; analogy from one revolution to the other; and intellectual development in the form of major ideas and new perspectives on man, society and history. The confluence of these three rays of light has produced a plethora of theories of social revolutions at one point or another. Each theory is distinguished from each other in essential suggestions, epistemological assumptions and the social context of intellectual origins.

The social context of the theorists of revolution such as Aristotle, Machiavelli, Hobbs and Marx, for example, was characterized by the rise and fall of city-states, princes, communities and ruling classes. Similarly, the scene surrounding contemporary theorists—who are too numerous to name—is typified by revolutions in Asia, Africa, Latin America and the Middle East.

---

* Department of Sociology, University of Wyoming, Laramie, U.S.A.

Revolution is a catchword in our times, and there are visible signs of change
in the social structure everywhere, either in altered cultural traditions, altered
economic relations or altered political order.

The interpretation of historical epochs, the French, Russian and Chinese
revolutions, and also perhaps the Renaissance and Reformation, influenced
our thinking about revolution. The echo of earlier revolutions, in Marx's
pejorative statement, becomes parody in later ones. "Revolutions give rise to
myths", George Lichtheim (1964:52) argued, "and these myths then help to
shape the course of later revolutions." One revolution is analogous to another,
according to those who see a distinct pattern in the Great Three social revolutions. Albert Sorel once wrote: "Consider the revolutions of the Renaissance.
In them you will find all the passions, all the spirit, and all the language of the
French Revolution." (cited by Deutscher 1952: 369). Frederick Engels
declared that "Russia was the France of the new age." He expected another
1789 and alluded to the same passions, spirit and language of the French
Revolution. (Deutscher 1952: 369).

Images are products of intellectual development. They are intellectual acts
involving a change in the way we look at things. The image of revolution has
changed in accordance with the change in man's conception of history. The
classic view of history as a cyclical flow of random events was supplemented,
if not supplanted, by a radical conception of history as an evolutionary,
cumulative path of progress. The image of revolution also changed along with
changing models of society as either organismic, mechanistic, or cybernetic
(see Deutsch 1963). Whether social order or social change is assumed to be
given or questioned as a serious topic of inquiry shapes our images of revolution. So does whether society is viewed as a holistic entity or state is considered
as an independent force of history. Another source of change was the alteration
in the models of man as proactive agent of history, seeking to change the given
conditions with will and consciousness, or as reactive stimulus-response slot
machine to social forces of frustration and gratification.

The oldest and classic image of revolution is as a revolving wheel of
history. It is reflected in Polybius' account of the rise and fall of the Greek city-
states and Aristotle's cyclical theory of history. Aristotle viewed revolution as
a ceaseless cycle between the rule of the one, the few and the many.

The image of revolution as a cyclical change of political regimes or
dynasties as in the Chinese historiography, is directly related to the origin of
the term, which was first used in astrology. Astrology sought to forecast fateful
events by the approaching conjunctions of the planets, the movements of which
were designated by the late-Latin coinage *revolutiones*. Though the revolutions
of the planets implied in general a return of favorable or unfavorable influences
to a previous aspect—as in the Chinese word for revolution, a change in the
mandate of heaven—the revolution of politics more specifically referred to a
sudden reversal of fate: the fall of the mighty or the elevation of the oppressed.
Both meanings co-existed in the word that was subsequently to be borrowed
by all European and, in our time, non-European languages. (see Friedrich
1966).

Revolutions, according to this image, were little more than a change of persons, or an alteration of local circumstances. Furthermore, political revolutions, like astronomical revolutions, are thought to be beyond human control. They rise and fall in the course of things, and they produce only transitory changes in the form of government and in the conditions of inequality between economic and political power.

Most revolutions prior to 19th century were conservative, even reactionary, trying to restore a former situation, real or imagined. They called for the preservation of order and religion and protection of property. In other words, the government might change and the group in power might represent different interests, but its objective was not to rush headlong into a totally new and unfamiliar future. They tried to solidify the past and halt the abrupt flow of history.

This conception of revolution as a process of ordering finds its expression in the English Civil War. In England in the 1660s, "revolution" meant the restoration of the monarchy, not at all the acts of Cromwell and his government, but the overthrow of the Rump Parliament. In 1688, the expulsion of the Stuarts and the crowning of William and Mary came to be called a revolution. Known as the "Glorious Revolution", it was in fact a reinstatement of the power of the monarchy in its pristine glory, which disorders had ruined. (see Childs 1980; Miller 1983).

The French revolution replaced the image of the turning wheel with that of the watershed. The 1789 French revolution was considered as a "summary and the last formula of an expiring age." (Mazzini 1912: 251). The new element here is the progressive notion of history. For the first time, the idea of revolution as an end of an age and beginning of a new era came to prevail. It was taken up and given new depth and impetus by Marx and Engels.

Revolution for Marx is a historical category. The whole of his theory of revolution is set in the frame of a progressive conception of history and man. His theory of society is a society-in-history, and his theory of revolution is a theory of the transformation of society in history. Aristotle viewed revolution as a transitory process from aristocracy to oligarchy, from oligarchy to democracy, and possibly from democracy to oligarchy or monarchy. Marx saw each revolution instead as a historical progression from feudal society to capitalist society, and then to socialist and finally communist society. The axial principle of revolutionary changes lies not in political superstructure but in economic production and organization. The transition from one type of economic-social-political system to another may be violent. In fact, it is invariably violent because "the ruling class defends its position battling the other class historically destined to succeed it."

Revolution involves the appropriation of the man-produced world of material objects that Marx described in his early writings as "anthropological nature", or "the nature produced by history." In Marx's words, "the whole of history is nothing but a continual transformation of human nature." ([1847] 1956: 160). What is fundamentally at issue in the class struggle and in social revolution, as in history as a whole, is not the consumption interest but the production interest—defined in a special Marxist way. It is man as frustrated producer rather than man as dissatisfied consumer who makes a revolution. The source of revolutionary energy in a class is the frustration of man in his capacity of producer, his inability to develop new powers of production to the full within the confines of an existing mode of production or socio-economic order. The bourgeois revolution, for example, results from the inability of the rising capitalist class to develop the new productive powers within the cramping confines of feudal relationships.

For Marx, the change in the mode of production is both the cause and effect of revolution. It is something occurring when a form of society nears its end. "No social order ever disappears", Marx wrote, "before all the productive forces for which there is room in it, have developed; and new higher relations of production never appear before the material conditions of their existence have matured in womb of the old society." ([1859] 1970: 183). Historical development which leads to revolution is in itself inevitable, and revolution is predictable because the processes of history follow certain scientifically determined lines.

Until the 18th century, it was on rare occasions that men preoccupied themselves with the nature of revolution. When they did—as Machiavelli, Bodin and Hobbes did—it was with the intent of finding ways to prevent popular unrest, to maintain authority and to quell disorder. Revolution was looked upon as a political accident. It was not studied for its own sake, and it was certainly not desirable. But intellectuals of the 19th century revolving around the Marxist thoughts saw that revolution could be appraised and analyzed after the fact in order to enrich the body of human thought. According to this early intellectual tradition, a revolution is a compressed evolution. It is not measured by the nature of events but by the final results. Any deep-rooted transformation of social structure is tantamount to revolution. This view was an obvious analogy to the "industrial revolution" which these 19th century themselves experienced. (Ellul 1971).

Many intellectuals of the 19th century recognized that the transition from a rural agricultural society to an urban industrial one entailed a profound change in patterns of existence, in customs and in standards of value and it left no segment of society untouched or unaltered. Such a vast and penetrating transformation suggested effects comparable to those of a revolution, and for linguistic convenience, the description was abbreviated to "industrial revolution." Intended as a metaphor, the phrase then came into common use, the quotation marks disappeared, and the words were taken at their value. Ever since, revolution is anything that, like the industrial revolution, entails radically substantial change in the social structure.

Frequently, innovations in natural and biological sciences have found their way into social sciences and have affected the mode in which revolution has been conceived. Marx's image of revolution as historical catharsis and social advancement, for example, is an obvious manifestation of Darwinism. A relatively secular social structure and widespread belief in individual achievement have reinforced the atmosphere of faith in progress from the 18th century until our day. In this tradition, the act of revolution now often seems to represent no more than a penstroke eliminating every obstacle to progress. The image has been intensified by the Newtonian mechanics, by the assurance of control over nature and by the conception of society as a species of nature with independent laws that must be recognized and observed, just like laws in the physical world. Furthermore, the idea that society, like nature, can be acted upon through technical means, has created an image of revolution as a form of legitimate human endeavor. The analogy between nature and society, between natural science and politics, accounts for the modern glorification of revolution.

Approaches toward the study of revolution in a social scientific manner emerged in the latter part of the 19th century as intellectuals began to grapple with the problems of understanding social change. Weber, Durkheim, Pareto and Toennies, among others, introduced a sociological framework, consisting of analytical categories. While Marx saw society in history, these early sociologists saw history through sociological categories. Revolution in this view can be described, explained and even predicted, depending on the power of these analytical categories to identify causal relations among social factors. According to Weberian thinking, for instance, the causes of social order and social change are not to be found in one particular economic system, i.e., capitalism, but in the relationship among the economic system, political structure and cultural values over time. Disorder is seen as stemming from the lag between culture and technology and the resulting loss of legitimacy and power of the government. Revolution is a reaction to, or assualt upon, the power structure and reconstitution of it. The dominant force that mobilizes people to act is not so much material interest as such but values that works like a switchman in history. As analytical tools for the study of social change, Durkheim introduced a dichotomy between mechanical solidarity based on ascriptive social ties and organic solidarity constructed on an achievement-oriented division of labor. Social integration depends on collective conscience. As societies become more complex, more roles become differentiated from each other. Value consensus is the glue that ties people in diverse roles together and makes society possible. When it is broken, anomie—normlessness—prevails and leads to social disintegration.

In the 1960s several influences shaped the study of revolutions: the development and application of structural-functionalism in sociology and political science; the reflections on the breakup of colonial empires and the rise of independent states in the Third World and concerns for their political development; and scientific culture that demands precision, verification and explanation in the disciplines. All of these created what one can call the society-centered ''societal'' paradigm.

The most representative works in structural-functional tradition are Smelser's *Theory of Collective Behavior* (1962) and Johnson's theory of *Revolu-*

tionary Change (1966). Smelser organizes the causes of collective behavior in terms of six determinants: structural conduciveness, structural strain, generalized beliefs, precipiating factors, mobilization for action and social control. The final outcome depends on how each determinant combines with the previous ones in a "value-added" form. Smelser's distinction between collective behavior and social movements is based on types of generalized beliefs; for example, there are two kinds of social movements: norm-oriented and value-oriented. According to Johnson, a revolution is a state of social change brought about by multiple dysfunction in society, the act of revolt itself being precipitated by identifiable "accelerators."

In a similar vein, Gurr (1968; 1970) cast a wide net that attempts to capture "the basic preconditions for civil strife of any kind" (1968: 1104) with the concept of relative deprivation. Relative deprivation is the "actors' perceptions of discrepancy between their value expectations and their value capabilities." (1968: 1104).

In political science, Almond (Almond and Coleman 1960) pioneered a structural-functional approach out of the recognition that "politics in developing areas do not follow legal or customary norms defining the powers of various institutions. Hence, the properties of institutions were not taken as normatively given but as something to be researched empirically. And particularly if one wanted to compare political systems across cultures, one had to examine functions as well as normative and legal structure." (Almond 1988: 868). The general view of the social change in developing areas was that these countries are modernizing out of the traditional past into the modern form that is politically democratic and culturally rational like those supposedly to be found in the industrialized West. Their political instability was seen as a kind of inevitable transitory anomaly of modernization.

Critics have found it impossible to identify all of Smelser's stages in some episodes of collective behavior (see for e.g., Quarantelli and Hundley 1969; Marx and Wood 1975). A major reason for this problem is that the determinants are so vague and general that it is hard to establish their presence. Smelser fails to consider whether, for example, generalized belief is important for actors in a given collective event, and whether the emergence of new norms in collective processes is less important than development of new social relationships. The idea of a value-added system is too simple and rigid, and even misleading, for it implies a linear development of collective behavior, and ignores a complex and paradoxical interplay of cumulative effects of social control and other determinants. To be sure, each determinant sets the limits within which the next one can operate, but each stage can change, as authorities and social actors to change the conditions in their favor. The value-oriented collective behavior is unsatisfactory in explaining revolutionary movement, because the concepts are not sharply delineated to fit concrete historical situations, and the model does not explain how a revolt becomes successful or fails. It is not easy to define or set up the empirical conditions under which the theory can be tested. The complexity of most episodes of collective behavior makes it hard to prove Smelser's theory true or false, and because it cannot be proved true or false, the value of the theory as a source of hypothesis is somewhat limited. (see Marx and Wood 1975). The concept of strain, for example, is difficult to measure, and other specific propositions, though insightful and systematic, do not easily lend themselves to rigorous measurement. The scheme is devoid of the role of violence and the impact of its timing upon the authority of the power structure and the legitimacy of social forces.

Similar criticisms can be applied to the works represented by Johnson (1966) and Gurr (1970). The crucial variables such as "disequilibrium" and "system frustration" are vague and ambiguous, difficult to measure and observe in practice. The outcomes to which these analyses allude are also vague and do not distinguish between collective violence, domestic turmoil, and political instability from specifically revolutionary situation.

The "functions" that Almond and others have assumed as prerequisites for political systems were thinly disguised abstractions from the "liberal" interpretation of U.S. politics where plural interest groups compete for influence and power. (see Fabbrini 1988; Skocpol 1988). Huntington (1968) offered a somewhat realistic perspective on the politics of developing areas. Instead of looking for the functional equivalents of "interest articulation" and "interest aggregation," as Almond and Coleman (1960) did, he viewed Third World politics as revolutionary struggles for state power by radically discontended social forces—workers, students, urban "middle classes," peasants, etc. He proposed explanations why, for example, pressures for change assumed a reformist or revolutionary character, why reforms or revolutions succeeded or failed, and why, in the absence of either reform or revolution, some Third World countries become authoritarian. Modernization, especially the disjunctive rates of change between economic forces and political institutions, breeds revolution.

Tilly (1975) offered a different view and scheme for the analysis of revolution from a historically informed position. He rejected the thesis that modernization breeds revolution. (Tilly 1973). Instead, the conflict between social forces and the state does. He also rejected the societal approach where there is no history and no analytical distinction between society and the state. He saw revolution as the fragmentation of a single polity into more than one, a situation he called "multiple sovereignty." It begins when some people defy the authority, establish an alterantive authority and compel people to obey the alternative authority. There is a struggle for power between contenders and authorities over resources. It continues until only one central authority remains.

Tilly recognized, however, that it is difficult to develop "a reliable procedure for enumerating contenders, measuring their mobilization, and characterizing their relationship to the existing structure of power" in concrete historical circumstances. (see Rule and Tilly 1972). In fact, contenders and challengers for power are difficult to observe and measure because one has to infer dubious intentions from the actors from publically available sources. The idea that resources determine the outcomes of revolutionary movements is difficult to verify because observing and measuring resources cannot be standardized systematically across cultures and history. The emphasis on the intentions of revolutionaries as the cause and energy of revolution is overdrawn.

The central tenet of a societal paradigm of revolution is this:

> First, changes in social systems or societies give rise to grievances, social disorientation, or new class or group interests and potentials for collective mobilization. Then there develops a purposive, mass-based movement—coalescing with the aid of ideology and organization—that consciously undertakes to overthrow the existing government and perhaps the entire social order. Finally, the revolutionary movement fights it out with the authorities or dominant class and, if it wins, undertakes to establish its own authority and program. (Skocpol 1979: 14-15).

The studies of revolution have reached a new level of sophistication as a result of the critical evaluation of Marxist views on revolution and social change. Marxists interpreted the French Revolution, for instance, as an epic of the class struggle in which the feudal order was replaced by a financial and industrial bourgeoisie on the basis of an alliance between the middle class and the emerging urban proletariat. Historical studies (See Cobban 1964; Cobb 1972; Furet 1981) have largely refuted this claim. Historians hold that the feudal regime died out long before 1789. The "bourgeoisie" did not make the revolution. It was not the urban poor who overturned the existing power structure but the rural masses. As Alexis de Tocqueville suggested in 1856, the revolution was a reaction to the centralization of state power. Barrington Moore, Jr. (1966), for example, carried the Marxist thesis into a political analysis and found from his comparative studies that a class coalition, not just a class—either proletariat or bourgeoisie—in conflict or cooperation with the state, determined either the democratic or dictatorial form of governments in industrial societies. Reflections on the problems of advanced industrial societies in light of "orthodox" Marxism produced critical "revisions" and rethinkings of Marxism as a useful theory. For instance, students of revolution found Marxist theories lacking in explanatory power because they do not accord autonomy to state structures and politics.

Theda Skocpol's *States and Social Revolutions* (1979) is the exemplar of the new statist paradigm, a shift from both structural functional and Marxist views. Marx argued that the social existence of men determines their consciousness. From that point of view, "reality" is the material substructure of society and all the rest—laws, religion, politics, philosophy—is the superstructure. The change in the material substructure shapes the changes in the superstructure. Skocpol modified the order of primacy and freed herself from the class determinism of Marxism: politics takes command of history. The means and relations of power and authority, instead of the means and relations of production, determine social change. She writes:

> We can make sense of social transformations only if we take the state seriously as a macrostructure. The state properly conceived is no mere arena in which socio-economic struggles

are fought out. It is rather a set of administrative, policing, and military organizations headed, and more or less coordinated by, an executive authority. (1979: 29).

She argues that social order does not rest upon a consensus of the majority. Regimes survive even if the needs of the people are not met. Repressive and illegitimate regimes such as South Africa can and do survive.

She rejects the voluntary theory of revolution. "No single acting group," she maintains, "whether a class or an ideological vanguard, deliberately shapes the complex and multiply determined conflicts that bring about revolutionary crises and outcomes." (1985: 86-87) "Revolutions are not made by an aggregate of discontented people. Nor by organized groups with access to some resources. They do not erupt of 'system disequilibrium' deligitimation of authority and ideological conversion to revolutionary world views. They come." (1979: 15-17) The causes of revolutions are to be found in "the objective relationships and conflicts among variously situated groups and nations, rather than the interests, outlooks or ideologies of particular actors in revolutions." (1979: 291). Revolutions owe their success more to the paralysis of the state than to the power of revolutionary groups.

Skocpol (1979) asks why revolutions occurred in France, Russia and China, but not in Prussia, Japan or England. Her answer is that the weakness of the state, caused by bureaucratic/landed class conflict, precipitated by international pressures, prompted peasant revolts that overwhelmed the former, but not the latter. For her, the state power is both the cause and effect of revolution. A successful revolution creates and institutionalizes a new political order. It is more centralized than the regime it replaced. Its power is based on expanded mass mobilization and thus stronger than before.

The state-centered paradigm was built on the weakness of the society-centered approach. Now the role of the state, the relationship between the political elites and the other classes, international impact upon the state, and the institutional strength of the armed forces and the bureaucracy, instead of domestic social factors, are the crucial explanatory variables of revolutionary outbreaks and outcomes.

In recent years, however, there have been several criticisms against the statist paradigm. To be sure, states can be strong or weak, and states can be more or less autonomous. States also vary in terms of coercive, extractive, regulative, allocative or distributive capabilities. It is not clear, critics argue, what stateness includes or excludes, what the exhaustive dimensions of the state are. It is difficult to measure the strength and autonomy of the state. State, like power, is an ambiguous concept (see Almond 1988; Clark and Lemco 1988), but an indispensable tool for analysis of revolution.

The explanatory power of Skocpol's model is limited to a few specific historical cases and range of outcomes. The model does not explain why some revolutions produced dictatorship and others democracy, bourgeois or socialist outcomes, why private property was consilidated in one country and abolished in another.

Critics have also complained that her treatment of the role of ideology in revolution is inadequate and her rejection of culture as irrelevant to revolutionary activities is misleading. Sewell (1985), for instance, highlights the autonomous power of ideology in the revolutionary process of the 1789 France in contrast to Skocpol's interpretation. Arjomand (1986) argues that ideology and culture were crucial in the Iranian revolution in evaluating the exercise of the authority, inspiring rebellion, mobilizing, organizing and leading the oppositions, and shaping the nature of the post-revolutionary state.

Her emphasis on structural features led to an over-deterministic view of history. What people did or did not do, did not matter. Revolutions are like a hurricane. Men and women, like leaves in the wind, are swept away by the impersonal power of historic proportion. Historians saw it differently. The essential feature of the Russian Revolution, for instance, was the leadership of an ideologically conscious *avant-garde* with the mass party as its instrument, and the basic objective of the struggle was for the state power. The Chinese Revolution was also the work of an effective leadership. This leadership utilized the discontent of the hitherto unmobilized peasants, as Benjamin Schwartz (1951) suggested. It also exploited the alliance between the peasants and the urban intelligentsia which was cemented by nationalism. The Russian and Chinese cases show that a specifically organized and disciplined group of men, willed and conscious, can destroy the established order and reconstruct society according to their choice.

In the statist model, the revolutionary process is unidimensional, that is, something that does not vary and is beyond human control. Thus, the theoretical connection between the origins and outcomes is shortcircuited. There is no discussion on the unfolding of the revolutionary process, how and why different social forces participate at different points in time, and the causes and effects of the interaction between the state and social forces during the revolutionary process. All the revolutions were inevitable. Reform or repression, actions by elites to forestall revolutions were inconsequential. This position, I think, is untenable.

The methodology Skocpol applies to the analysis of revolutions has its strengths and limitations. Historical methods offer a rich and detailed information for analysis. Contrasting differences and similarities make componential features and configurations very clear. The methodological canons of the comparative-historical method are chronological order and time-place unity. What happened earlier determines what comes later. Particular nations constitute irreducible wholes and unique sociohistorical configurations in their own right. Explanations are derived from combining temporal and geographical components.

As Skocpol herself recognizes, historical analyses, however, do not validate a theory. Juxtaposed historical trajectories are not used to establish controls, only to show the theory at work (see Skocpol and Somers 1980). "Because they are largely inductively established, comparative-historical causal arguments cannot be readily generalized beyond the cases actually discussed." (Skocpol and Somers 1980: 195). The task of truly explanatory theories is to break apart temporal and geographical unities and provide links among valid causal generalizations about different sets of times and places. The statist-structural approach does not offer a general theory of revolution. The challenge to do so is extended to all serious students of revolution.

Reflections on and analyses of the Iranian revolution contradict many of her arguments. The weakness of the state did not prompt revolution in Iran. There were no financial and fiscal crises. The conscientious urban forces rather than structural rural elements significantly contributed to the outbreak and outcome of the revolution. Liu (1988: 179) argues that "in contrast to the Great French, Russian, and Chinese revolutions, [the Iranian] state broke down without massive peasant mobilization and revolts in the countryside." It was primarily an urban revolt. "The Shiite clergy rallied the bazaar classes, the modern classes, the industrial workers, the urban poor, and all political groups against the monarchy. Revolution was made. It did not come." (Liu 1988: 179). Domestic social factors and relative deprivation were indispensable in accounting for the revolution. Arjomand (1986), for instance, argues that socially dislocated and culturally disoriented individuals found in the Shiite Islam an integrative moral force from which the Iranian revolutionary movements were forged. "The conspicuous consumption on the part of Iranian high society and the abundance of *nouveaux riches* produced an acute sense of relative deprivation among the new middle class, government employees, white-collar workers in the private sector, and schoolteachers." (Arjomand 1986: 397). These people all supported the militant clerics against the shah.

The timing of the revolutionary outbreak was related to relative deprivation. In 1962, James Davies suggested that the Marxist notion that revolutions result from increasing economic degradation and Tocqueville's theory that they are products of an improving economic situation are equally valid. Revolutions, he contended, in fact occur when Tocqueville's scenario is followed by Marx's: they are produced when long-term economic advancement is followed by a sudden and short episode of decline, known as the J-curve theory of revolution. "Iran's GNP grew by 30.3 percent in 1973-1974 and by a further 42 percent in 1974-75. Then came the economic debacle, despite, or rather because of, the massive unregulated inflow of oil revenue." (Arjomand 1986: 397). Arjomand argues that there was a widespread discontent in 1977-1978 in Iran. Even though we may not accept the psychological interpretation, we cannot ignore the correlation between the J-curve and the violent political outbreaks.

The collected essays in this volume reflect the difficulties of the societal and statist perspectives in explaining a wide range of revolutionary phenomena. The approaches that contributors use in their analyses combine critically and creatively theoretical strands of both perspectives. Their approaches also reflect disciplinary diversity. They do share, however, a structural perspective. They show historical traditions, political culture and ideology, public opinion, relative deprivation, resources, public campaigns, state structures and interna-

tional relations are important in accounting for the origins, processes and outcomes of revolutionary movements.

The countries in Asia, Africa, Latin America and the Middle East have
undergone revolutionary changes during the last half a century in almost all
aspects of the lives of the people. One of the most profound and dramatic
changes has been and continues to be the institutions that govern the relationship between the rulers and ruled. The struggle to shape their own destiny is
going on and will continue. The revolutionary movements of this kind are
complex, but they are patterned by historical and structural factors beyond
individual comprehension and control. The essays contribute to a theoretical
and empirical understanding of the forces that make up the movements. A
wide range of topics with different degrees of focus on revolutionary activites
are discussed in this volume. They range from protest movements, civil strife,
military *coup d'etat*, rebellion to revolution.

The cases discussed here, regretfully, represent only a small, unrepresen-
tative sample of the wide and diverse universe of revolutionary movements in
the Third World. Studies on Mexico and Vietnam, for example, are missing,
so is Peru and South Africa, to name only a few. Neither in theoretical nor
empirical level are the contributions of these studies complete. They do, however, direct our attention to a new paradigm that could combine both the
societal and statist perspectives.

Will Moore and Keith Jaggers discuss the theoretical issues of synthesizing
a conceptual model across different levels of analysis. The three focuses—
group, organization and nation-state—and the corresponding theories around
these levels can complement rather than contradict each other and can produce
useful explanations of why men take up arms against the state. They suggest
that people come to act together in defiance against the authority not only on
the basis of pre-existing social ties but also on a common platform of anger and
views of what should be done. Actions and inactions of the authorities determine the mobilization of groups. Appeals of various kinds, and coordinating
activities and public campaigns, link the individuals to the collective entity
which can and often does undermine state power. They write: "When
individuals realize that private grievances are collectively shared, they are
likely to gain courage to solve them collectively." Contrary to what one would
expect from a rational theory (see, for example, Olson 1965; Popkin 1979;
Taylor 1988), they show that there are political entrepreneurs who initiate collective mobilization and act on moral grounds other than individual self-
interests.

Jeffery Paige critically reviews Barrington Moore Jr.'s class-centered
theory of revolution in light of the revolutionary experiences, or the lack
thereof, and political outcomes in Central American countries including El
Salvador, Costa Rica and Nicaragua. He finds that the Central American
bourgeoisie did not support democratic revolution but were more likely to back
authoritarianism. Bourgeouis support for even limited democracy was highly
contingent upon and related to the absence of serious challenge from below.

Moore's thesis, "no bourgeoisie, no democracy" needs to be reconsidered in light of the political histories of El Salvador, Costa Rica and Nicaragua. He maintains that "imperial control, not traditional agrarian bureaucracy, critically weakened the bourgeoisie and opened the way for socialist revolution, and these revolutions were a result of capitalist pulverization of the peasantry, not the persistence of cohesive peasant villages."

José Moreno presents a historical analysis of the relationship between the Caribbean countries and the Western powers on how dependent relations constrain any attempt to change the existing class structure. He shows that the "successful" revolutions in Haiti in 1804 and Cuba in 1959 were possible only when dependency ties with France and the United States respectively were broken. In contrast, the revolutionary movement of the Dominican Republic in 1965 failed and prompted the U.S. military intervention due to strong dependency relations between the two countries.

Quee-Young Kim presents a case study in which a protest movement turned into a revolution. To the amazement of many, including the participants and authorities, a series of street demonstrations escalated into a major violent conflict between various social forces and the Syngman Rhee regime in South Korea in 1960 and ultimately overthrew the regime. I develop a conceptual model both inductively and deductively using, instead of impersonal objective patterns of state variables, public opinion and consciousness as explanatory factors. The root cause of the upheaval was an acute sense of injustice that contradicted the principles of legitimacy of the government. I call it "disjunctive justice." The disjunctive justice, however, did not lead directly to protest movements. Individuals with organizational network and some real or imagined support from the public and access to the mass media inspired students to stage protest movements. Rhee's police responded to demonstrations with force, thus galvanizing the opposition and actually strengthening it. The massacre of demonstrators increased the anger of the common citizens. The government declared martial law and relied upon the military to quell the upheaval. More massive demonstrations were in the offing and the military would not and could not "fire upon the students" because an overwhelmingly supportive public opinion was behind the cause. The regime fell, contrary to the original intentions of the protesters themselves. Though many protest movements fail, the upheaval succeeded beyond anyone's expectation. In general, I argue that protest movements stem from the political and moral interactions between the society and the state and the analysis of revolutionary movements must contrast the society and the state in a dialectical relationship.

Yossi Shain and Mark Thompson highlight the role of exiles in undermining the legitimacy of a dictatorial regime. They recognize that democratic transitions of authoritarian regimes in Southern Europe, Latin America and recently in East Asia have been motivated and shaped by socio-political factors within the society, but when opposition groups are suppressed inside the country, the movement can and and often does continue abroad. They document the opposition movement against Marcos, especially the role of the Fillipino dissidents in the United States and the making of an incipient "counter-government".

Brigid Starkey emphasizes the role of "cultural orientations" in the genesis of the Iranian revolution in which a combination of religious heterodoxy, demands for equality and justice, and political rebellion transformed the regime. She argues that "while the state must be considered an important object of analysis, in the Iranian case more emphasis must be placed on culture as a specific level of analysis." She sees culture not as "values and belief systems" but as "the vehicle and product of the search for intersubjective meanings," a kind of idiom that lends meaning to political language and inspires political action. The Islamic idiom provided the tools for action.

Farideh Farhi sees the Iranian revolution basically as an ideological revolution and considers ideology a glue that binds the society and state together. Two ideologies contradicted each other: the Pahlavi's ideology composed of official nationalism, pre-Islamic grandeur and the defense of the monarchy as the true representative of progressive, modernizing and democratizing forces; and religious ideology composed of Islamic nationalism and Khomeni's theocratic interpretation of the role of the clergy. Rapid social change, economic downturns and absurd political leadership galvanized the ideological contradictions and inspired a vision of new community through a recomposition of Islamic ideology.

Finally in the selection, Quee-Young Kim and Jennifer Leach examine the two dominant types of revolution in Africa (military *coup d'etat* and revolution from above) by comparing and contrasting the recent histories of Ethiopia and the Sudan. We found that the institutional autonomy and coherence of the military and of the centralized bureacratic apparatuses made a crucial difference in their attempts at revolution. The ability to institutionalize structural changes varied depending upon the social, religious and ethnic support that the new state could create, however.

The paradigm of revolution has gone through several transformations. So has the meaning of revolution. Paradigms change not because a certain theory proved to be false but because new students ask new questions. New forms of revolution occur to compel the revision of old views. Revolutions in modern times have occurred in more complex national and international settings than those in the 18th and 19th centuries; their forms were varied and the effects complex. Revolutions mean not just a violent change of government but, as well, extensive social transformation and radical actions to bring about changes in leadership, policies, institutional arrangements and class structure. We are not only interested in whether a specific revolution has succeeded or failed but also whether that revolution will produce a dictatorship or democracy; what kinds of effects the revolution from below will create as opposed to revolution from above; once a protest movement occurs, what will make it turn into a revolutionary movement; and the probabilities of institutionalizing a revolution despite of some international pressures. In short, we are interested in the causes, processes and outcomes of various forms of revolutionary movements such as protests, strikes, *coups d'etat*, revolts, rebellions and revolutions.

The two main paradigms of revolution, the societal and statist, have their strengths and weaknesses. The former can explain a wide variety of revolutionary events with a few variables while the latter can interpret the causes and outcomes of specific historical revolutions. The societal approach, however, puts too much emphasis on grievances as the cause of all kinds of defiant actions and does not pay enough attention to the study of the processes and the outcomes of revolutionary actions. The statist approach stresses too much the importance of the coercive and extractive capabilities of the state and focuses too narrowly on the strength and weakness of the politico-military organizations.

Both views lack explanatory power due to "structural" bias and a lack of cultural insights. Different social actions can arise under identical social structure and different social structures can produce identical social action because men and women of different cultures justify and explain their social action differently. Both paradigms need to be transformed into something that is able to explain a wide range of revolutionary activities with greater precision. Too much emphasis on one at the expense of the other violates, fundamentally, the ontological distinctions among society, polity and culture. Each responds to different norms, has different rhythms of change and is regulated by different even contrary principles. (See Weber ([1921] 1968 and Bell 1976).

Culture, like state, is a crucial concept for the analysis of revolution. Culture is a "tool kit" for constructing "strategies of action," rather than a switchman directing an engine propelled by interests (Swidler 1986). Using culture in this way, we can explain why different groups behave differently in the same structural situation and the extent of continuities or discontinuities in action in the face of structural changes. In "settled lives," according to Swidler, culture and structural circumstances reinforce each other as institutionalized ethos. In "unsettled lives"—the periods of social transformation— cultural models, such as ideologies, play a powerful role in organizing social life. (Swidler 1986: 278).

The state is crucial in any analysis of revolutionary movements. States vary in their structures and relations to society, and thus differ in their ability to manage revolutionary challenges. The state can be viewed as an institutional and legal order with coercive, extractive, regulative and distributive powers, structured on historically determined, socio-economically contingent, organizing principles. According to Fabbrini (1988: 896),

> [These organizing principles] are visible principles in the sense that they institutionalize themselves in norms, regulations, procedures, resources, and relations; and public action must therefore be conducted within the constraints and opportunities defined by the characteristics of that process of institutionalization.

The ability of oppositions to challenge the authorities depends on resources and organizations while the quality and quantity of conflict and public support and leadership determine the outcome. Revolution then is a dialectical process between deinstitutionalization of state power and institutionalization of new social forces. Juxtaposing the state against the society, using culture and ideology as mediating variables, can perhaps lead to more interesting hypotheses and explain a wide range of possible outcomes and the origins, processes and outcomes of revolutionary movements. We hope that this volume and the dialectical view will help students of revolution analyze the phenomenon better and enlighten the readers about what are perhaps the most significant events of this modern century.

Deprivation, Mobilization and the State: A Synthetic Model of Rebellion

WILL H. MOORE and KEITH JAGGERS*

ABSTRACT

In this paper it is argued that it is theoretically more useful to synthesize socio-psychological, political conflict and structural-determinist approaches to explaining rebellion than to choose among them. Taken in isolation, each model presents necessary, but theoretically insufficient, explanations of the conditions that precipitate armed rebellion. To synthesize these approaches, we argue that while relative deprivation provides the psychological impetus for collective action, organized groups which can focus discontent determine its activation. In addition, state power plays a key role in determining the impact of popular insurrection.

WITHIN THE LITERATURE ON REBELLION and revolution there exists a diversity of opinion about the "best" theoretical framework to employ. This can be illustrated by examining a set of recent articles which review the literature on rebellion, revolution and social movements. Eckstein (1980) divides the literature into those studies that assume conflict is inherent in society and those that assume it is contingent upon human actions, arguing that the two approaches are fundamentally distinct and incompatible. Goldstone (1980) argues that a third generation of theories of revolution are superior to those that preceded them. McAdam (1982: 5-59), on the other hand, suggests that political opportunity theories have greater explanatory power than classical theories of collective behavior. Moreover, Jenkins (1983: 527) claims that the resource mobilization perspective has led to an underemphasis of the "social psychology of mobilization," while Tarrow (1988) claims that the new social movements literature has properly restored the "political" to its central explanatory role. The common thread that runs through these reviews is the characterization of the literature on revolution and rebellion as consisting of competing rather than complementary approaches. Scholars are talking past, rather than with, each other.

This raises the question: Can we talk meaningfully about a scientific understanding of the causes of domestic political violence? In other words, has the elaboration of diverse theories of violent collective action illuminated or muddled our knowledge of why people take up arms against the state? The scholarly communities' reaction to this plethora of approaches has led to

*   Center for Comparative Politics, Department of Political Science, University of Colorado, Boulder, CO 80309-0333.

internecine bickering between the various schools of theoretical and methodological thought. Instead of clarifying our understanding of rebellion and
revolution, this state of affairs has resulted in theoretical fragmentation and
dissension.

Sounding a different call from the scholars cited above, McAdam *et. al.*
(1988) suggest that, rather than debate the relative merits of distinct theoretical
approaches, a synthetic approach to the study of collective action is needed.
In this paper we respond to that challenge by suggesting that it is to the benefit
of those who are interested in explaining the outbreak of rebellion to narrow
the scope of the debate toward the end of performing comparable analyses and
engaging in what Kuhn (1962) would call "normal science."

Within the literature on rebellion and revolution it is possible to identify
three broad conceptual frameworks, each focusing on a different level of
analysis within which most theorists work: socio-psychological approaches,
political conflict approaches and structural-determinist approaches.[1] Socio-
psychological explanations of the outbreak of violent conflict focus on the
individual level of analysis. These analyses typically concern themselves with
why individuals participate in rebellion.[2] In contrast, political conflict explanations concentrate on the collective level of analysis. Focusing attention on the
resources of challenger groups and the state, theories in this framework
typically concern themselves with the strategies employed in the formation of
challenger coalitions and movements, and state responses.[3] Finally, structural-
determinist analyses concentrate on the social-structural level of analysis.
Theories in this framework typically ask: What structural factors lead to the
emergence of revolutionary situations? State structures, and the state's relations with dominant classes and other states in the international system are
considered to be the relevant explanatory variables.[4]

In this article we argue that it is essential to utilize *all three* levels of analysis
if we are to enhance our ability to understand and explain the manifestation
of armed rebellion in the societies which populate our planet. We recognize
that one of the chief reasons scholars have chosen from among these
approaches is that none of the major theoretical frameworks adequately utilize
all three levels of analysis. By failing to do so, they leave us with a theoretically
fragmented understanding of the dynamics of rebellion and revolution.

Without examining the entire body of literature on rebellion and revolution,[5] we can highlight this problem by concentrating on the leading theoretical
treatise from each framework: Ted Gurr's *Why Men Rebel* (1970); Charles
Tilly's *From Mobilization to Revolution* (1978); and Theda Skocpol's *States and
Social Revolutions* (1979). These works are indicative of the civil strife literature
as a whole in that they tend to emphasize one level of analysis, relegating the
others to secondary or inconsequential roles. Thus, Gurr focuses on the
individual's motivation to take up arms against the state. Tilly, on the other
hand, is more concerned with the dynamics of group formation and mobilization than with individuals' psychological predispositions for violence. Finally,
Skocpol rejects what she calls the voluntarist arguments of both Gurr and
Tilly, arguing that revolutions are not made, they simply come.

Despite the obvious tensions among these works, the question remains: Are the barriers between them real or just the result of theoretical over-simplification by the theorists and the scholarly community? On closer examination, just because theories within each of these frameworks *focus* on one level of analysis does not mean that they necessarily restrict themselves to that level. For example, while Gurr (1970) concentrates on relative deprivation as a necessary condition for the outbreak of civil strife, he also cites the "coercive balance" between rebellious groups and the state, and the social-structural conditions which affect the outbreak of rebellion. Moreover, while Tilly (1978) focuses on group-state competition, that competition takes place in, and is constrained by, the structural conditions present within society. Finally, Skocpol (1979) stresses the importance of the structural causes of social revolutions. However, these structural conditions manifest themselves in inter-class conflict and conflict between those classes and a semi-autonomous state. Though these theorists may not want to admit it, these frameworks are not mutually exclusive.

A Theoretical Synthesis

The central thrust of this article is that Gurr (1970), Tilly (1978) and Skocpol (1979) can learn from each other. This does not suggest that the theories can be "pushed together" and a cogent synthesis will magically emerge. Nor does it deny that real tensions and debates exist among these works. Rather, we intend to elaborate those areas where the theories can complement each other, and demonstrate that a theoretical synthesis can be achieved. To retain our focus, we will address one central question: What is the process that results in individuals engaging in armed rebellion? In other words, *how* and *why* do people come together to challenge the existing regime? A theory that adequately addresses these questions must 1) account for an individual's willingness to expose himself or herself to exceptional physical danger, 2) explain how individuals come together to form rebel groups, and 3) reveal why groups of citizens are able to militarily challenge a state and its coercive apparatus. To address these questions, we propose a framework which elaborates the "micro-mobilization process" (Snow *et. al.* 1986) as the linkage between Tilly's (1978) discussion of categories, networks and group mobilization and Gurr's (1970) discussion of relative deprivation. Further, Gurr's (1970) notion of the "coercive balance" between rebels and states, and Tilly's (1978) discussion of state-challenger conflict is informed by Skocpol's state-centered analysis of the structural conditions which weaken a state's ability to employ its coercive capacity.

Groups: Categories and Networks

To create theoretical linkages between individual and group levels of analysis, rebel organizations must be conceptualized on both the individual and collective levels. While groups can be viewed as unitary collectivities systematically pursuing their goals through the process of organizational growth, they also must be conceptualized as concentrations of individuals who share common bonds and associational ties. To facilitate this integration of theoretical approaches, we begin with some definitions. At the individual level, a pool of potential rebels can be broken down into (1) those individuals who identify with the rebel group and are willing to act on that identification (i.e., adherents (McCarthy & Zald 1977)), (2) those individuals who identify but do not contribute (i.e., free-riders (Olson 1965)), and (3) those individuals who do not identify with the rebel group and, by default, are unwilling to act. The combined set of free-riders and those individuals who do not identify with the rebel group, we call potential group members (PGM's).

Moving to the collective level, groups can be further distinguished between (1) latent groups (Truman 1951) or unmobilized sentiment pools (McCarthy 1987), (2) organizations with potential for collective action (OPCA's), and (3) social movement organizations (SMO's (Zald & Ash 1966)). In this paper, we are only interested in groups which have formed a leadership core, therefore latent groups are not considered. The distinction between the latter two categories of collectivities is the level of mobilization they have attained. OPCA's have only the *potential* to act because they lack the requisite number and/or types of resources (i.e., ideological cohesion, material resources, human participation, communal structure/organization) necessary to act. Conversely, SMO's have both the number and types of resources necessary to act. This difference can be illustrated by the small band of FSLN guerrillas running around the Nicaraguan countryside in the late 1960s and early '70s, and the mass-based guerrilla organization that swept Somoza from power in July 1979.

The mobilization of *individual people* into *organized groups of people* (SMO's) should be a central explanatory variable in any theory of rebellion. The interaction between individuals and groups, in terms of recruitment and maintaining commitment of resources, are central theoretical issues. Yet, Gurr (1970) fails to adequately specify this process and Skocpol (1979) dismisses it as irrelevant. Tilly (1978), on the other hand, offers us guidance by elaborating the structure of group formation.

Borrowing from the work of Harrison White, Tilly defines groups as "a set of individuals comprising both a category and network." A network is made up "of people who are linked to each other, directly or indirectly, by a specific kind of interpersonal bond." (Tilly 1978: 62). On the other hand, a category is made up "of people who share some common characteristic," be it physical, ideological, or psychological (Tilly 1978: 62). Tilly then suggests that mobilization is a function of both categories and networks (or, cat-net). This view of mobilization is problematic because it is static; it compels us to define groups as *a priori* existent in society. Thus, the mobilization patterns in a society, and the groups they define, are given by the cat-net structure of that society. As a result, Tilly sees mobilization exclusively as a process where existing groups mobilize other groups to form larger groups; that groups also mobilize individuals is theoretically excluded. That resource mobilization theories have presented static analyses of mobilization has caused several scholars (Jenkins 1983, Klandermans 1984, McAdam *et. al.* 1988, and Snow *et. al.* 1986) to call for resource mobilization theorists to introduce some socio-psychological factors into their models. As Klandermans (1984 598) put it, "research on mobilization would do well to specify mobilization efforts."

We reject a static analysis of mobilization and introduce socio-psychological factors by focusing on the mobilization of both individuals and groups. Therefore, a given group's level of mobilization is not simply a function of the cat-net structures of society, but a function of that group's ability to exploit the cat-net structures present in society and forge new ones. As a result, categories and networks are important to our analysis of the transformation from latent groups to SMO's because "no matter how a typical participant describes his reasons for joining the movement, or what motives may be suggested by a social scientist on the basis of deprivation, disorganization, or deviancy models, it is clear that the original decision to join required some contact with the movement" (Gerlach and Hine 1970: p. 79). Thus, before an organization is capable of collective action, a salient category (important shared traits) *and* a strong network (frequent interaction) must both be present. If one, or both, are missing, they must be manufactured before an organization will be in a position to take collective action.

A potentially salient category with a weak national network is insufficient grounding for an effective national rebel organization because there is little or no communication among all members of the group, making it unlikely that they will act as a collective unit.[6] As Pinard (1971: 187) suggests, "[t]he higher the degree of social integration of potential adopters, the more likely and the sooner they will become actual adopters ... on the other hand, near-isolates tend to be the last to adopt an innovation." Moreover, not all members who belong to a particular category will necessarily find that category to be salient. In fact, people perceive themselves as members of several categories. However, a given individual is not likely to hold the same level of identification with all categories of which he or she is a member. Thus, one can postulate the existence of "preference rankings" over the categories with which an individual wishes to identify strongly versus those found lower in the ranking.

Similarly, an intrinsically strong network with a non-salient category is insufficient because there are no communal bonds among the members on which to build a formal organizational structure. Organizational structures are created to direct a group's action toward some common objective. However, as Ferree and Miller (1985: 46) suggest, "without a *homogeneous*, intensely interacting group ... people are unlikely to recognize that their private troubles are reflections of public issues rather than personal flaws."

In the final analysis, only when both a strong network and a salient category exist is a group capable of action. We are all familiar with categories of individuals which have a collective interest, yet do not act collectively. For example, when Zimbabwean nationalist guerrillas began military incursions into Rhodesia in the late 1960s, they were routed by Rhodesian Security Forces. This failure was attributed to a lack of support from the local African population in the areas they were active. While it is obvious that those local populations were members of the category the guerrillas purported to represent (i.e., Africans or Zimbabweans), the guerrillas had not established a network which brought those people into their group. As a result, the Zimbabwe African National Union (ZANU) sent groups of unarmed cadres into the Northeast region of Rhodesia over the next several years to gain the support of the local population by heightening the salience of their common "categoriness" and forging strong organizational ties between the guerrillas and the peasants. When ZANU reopened its guerrilla strategy in December 1972, the Rhodesian Security Forces were greatly dismayed at the lack of cooperation they received from the local African populations when trying to obtain intelligence on guerrilla activity and movement.[7] Given that rebel movements face these issues, two central questions emerge: How does a category become salient? and How do individuals develop an organizational network such that collective action becomes feasible? This is the topic addressed in the following section.

Micro-Mobilization: The Role of Appeals

Before one can measure the influence of group mobilization on the occurrence of civil strife, one must first understand the dynamics which draw individuals into these organizations and the process by which the pursuit of individual interests is translated into the pursuit of group interests. In short, without analyzing the impetus for individuals to join rebel groups that contend for power, the notion of groups as actors is nothing more than a theoretical abstraction with little explanatory power. This leads one to ask: How do groups persuade potential group members to commit their personal resources to the group? Snow et. al. (1986) refer to this process as "micro-mobilization" and suggest that groups must convince people that the group's "world-view"[8] is worth adopting. As important as this article is, the authors fail to explicitly elaborate the process by which groups "convince" people. We suggest that by issuing appeals, groups are able to "convince" people to adopt the group's "world-view," and thus mobilize them. Therefore, it is our contention that if groups of individuals are to effectively challenge the existing regime, they must issue appeals in an effort to mobilize those who have not decided to risk their lives in armed combat and prevent active members from leaving the guerrilla organization.

Building on Gurr (1970: 231), we have identified a five point typology of appeals used to mobilize individual discontent into rebel movements: (1) appeals to corporate identity, or "categoriness;" (2) appeals to an individual's sense of relative deprivation; (3) appeals that identify the existing regime as the source of that discontent; (4) appeals to normative justifications for taking violent action; and (5) appeals promoting the utilitarian value of rebellion. A brief examination of the literature demonstrates that this typology is supported by the observations of others.

Lenin (1929 and 1969) understood the importance of making appeals to corporate identity: i.e., "educating" the Russian proletariat about their common "categoriness." Where individuals already identify strongly with a given category, this problem does not exist. As a result, it was easier for the Muslim clergy in Iran to mobilize Islamic fundamentalists against the regime of Muhammed Reza Shah Pahlavi than it was for Lenin to mobilize the Russian working class against the Czar. To accomplish that shift in identification, Lenin created *ISKRA*, a revolutionary newspaper that was designed to educate and agitate the Russian working class. Of course, this method of disseminating appeals has been employed by most revolutionary movements in the Third World. Further, the printed word is supplemented with radio broadcasts from friendly states and clandestine meetings and rallies.

Snow *et. al.* (1986: 470) emphasize the importance of appeals to relative deprivation proposing that individuals must share the group's orientation toward greivances before they will become members. Schwartz (1971: 123) maintains that, in the case of rebellion, groups must focus the blame for the discontent on the state. Finally, that appeals to the normative justification for, and the utilitarian value of, collective action are necessary is supported by McAdam *et. al.* (1988: 722):

> [f]or the movement to succeed, it must be able to generate ... an ongoing sense of legitimacy and efficacy among movement cadre and members.

Thus, this typology of the appeals that rebel groups must issue in order to mobilize individuals is supported by a variety of scholars.

Yet, dividing these appeals into specific categories belies the interactive nature of reality. People do not consider whether their "world view" is aligned with that of a group in each of five categories; the process is much more holistic where categories overlap and complement each other. For example, the formation of corporate identity is the process by which an individual develops a fraternal identification with the group promoting rebellion. This is a process in which individuals come to realize a connection or sense of "commonality" with a larger group via their category. By promoting appeals to corporate identity, the core group is able to construct a psychological bond among individual potential group members, and a bond between them and the group itself.

It is the translation of individual deprivation into fraternalistic relative deprivation which enables the individual to articulate his or her frustrations in rebellious action:

> Unlike egoistic and individual deprivations, fraternalistic deprivation exists only among individuals who have a collective consciousness. By contrast, fraternalistic deprivation describes group deprivation sensed through comparisons made between one's in-group and other group's in the society; there is, however, no sense of deprivation concerning one's position within the in-group itself. (Sayles 1984: 452)

It is precisely this sense of *group interests*, based on a common identity of *fraternalistic relative deprivation*, which facilitates the organization of individuals into collective actors ready for mobilization against the perceived source of their discontent. In other words, if an individual perceives that his or her deprivation connects him or her with a larger group of individuals experiencing similar deprivation, then he or she is much more likely to join a group aimed at ameliorating individual deprivation. According to Sayles (1984: 452) a "collective consciousness may develop among individuals who share the same resentment (e.g., a group of economically deprived individuals), or it may develop among people with different resentments if they define themselves as having the same oppressor." In either case, it is evident that Gurr's (1970) relative deprivation model is a theoretically useful framework for helping to explain the entrance of individuals into group organizations. By showing that appeals provide a micro-mobilization linkage between the individual and collective levels of analysis, we have shown how the works of Tilly (1978) and Gurr (1970) can complement, rather than compete with each other.

Before we continue, it must be made explicit that while appeals to corporate identity attempt to transfer individual relative deprivation into a sense of fraternalistic relative deprivation, the existence of a high degree of individual relative deprivation must be maintained among group members. Without a continuing sense of individual relative deprivation, the ability of the group to mobilize collective participation in armed rebellion is severely constrained. This is because of the different types of resources fraternalistic and individual relative deprivation are likely to induce people to commit to the group. While fraternalistic relative deprivation will motivate potential group members to join a group, only when people experience high levels of individual relative deprivation will they be willing to commit their physical selves in conflict situations. In other words, individuals experiencing high levels of fraternalistic relative deprivation but low levels of individual relative deprivation will typically make economic or symbolic contributions to the group. However, as potential group members experience both fraternalistic and individual relative deprivation, they will become more likely to commit physical resources to the group as well as monetary and symbolic commitments.

For example, while many citizens of front-line African states feel a sense of fraternalistic deprivation with the ANC, they do not personally experience the individual deprivation that Africans in South Africa experience, which decreases the likelihood that they will join the ANC in armed struggle. Rather, they are more likely to donate money or lobby their governments to support the ANC in its struggle against apartheid. Similarly, several Americans were willing to open their pocketbooks for Oliver North to support the Contras in Nicaragua, but few were willing to join them in the jungle. While the value of monetary and symbolic contributions cannot be denied, a rebel movement without foot-soldiers is unlikely to make much progress toward overthrowing the state. While the convergence of a sense of fraternalistic relative deprivation is required for the process of group mobilization, only high levels of individual relative deprivation are likely to generate a group member's willingness to risk his or her life in armed rebellion. Without a high level of individual relative deprivation among the group members, the organization will disband when faced with a conflict situation. Thus, while fraternalistic relative deprivation facilitates group entrance, individual relative deprivation is the glue that bonds the group together in the face of adversity.

By positing the importance of appeals in the micro-mobilization process, a theoretical bridge is constructed to fill the gap left by both the socio-psychological and political conflict conceptual frameworks. This bridge assumes that while the individual is a primary unit of analysis, without the formation of "group consciousness" among these individuals, the likelihood of collective action is severely limited. In essence, the ability of groups to mobilize individual deprivation and channel this anger into organized movements vying for power is the heart of our synthesis. Thus, while groups provide the organizational means and spark for violent collective action, the deprivation found in the minds of people is the fuel of the revolutionary fire.

The Effectiveness of Appeals

To this point it has been argued that the *interaction* between relatively deprived individuals and organizationally adept groups explains how and why people engage in armed rebellion. Thus, we have assumed that appeals are effective in translating individual discontent into broad-based guerrilla organizations. Two questions are raised by the assumption that appeals are effective: (1) Why are appeals effective? and (2) How effective are they? To answer either question satisfactorily requires a systematic and detailed examination of the events and circumstances leading to conflict. Though such an examination is beyond the scope of this article, some suggestions are offered.

As noted above, people will identify more closely with some categories to which they belong than to others. For example, a Sikh living in India belongs to categories representing both his or her national affiliation and his or her ethno-religious affiliation. The same holds for Indians living in Peru, Eritreans in Ethiopia, Azerbaijanis and Georgians in the Soviet Union, and many others. In these situations, the state and the ethnic/religious group stake competing claims to that individual's resources. If an individual has not joined the rebel movement, the group must swing his or her identification preference to its side if it wishes to mobilize him or her. In short, rebel groups issue appeals designed to alter the preference rankings of those people who are members of the category they represent, but who have not joined the movement. To the extent that these appeals raise a potential group member's sense of fraternalistic and individual relative deprivation beyond some critical level, we can expect that individual to commit resources to the rebel movement. However, this does not necessarily mean that the preference ranking that person has for other groups he or she identifies with declines. It is possible for an individual to belong to several groups. Yet, given that people have a finite amount of personal resources, there is some level beyond which one group's demands begin to conflict with others. As a result, we expect that an increasing level of identification with an organization representing a new category will coincide with a decline in the level of identification with other groups.

The probability that appeals will effectively alter individuals' preference ranking structures can be analyzed from the standpoint of the types of categories to which they are issued, in conjunction with the types of deprivation they address. Categories can be divided into the following hierarchical classification: ethnic/religious and economic/political.[9] In addition, a distinction can be drawn between the extent of identification and the intensity of salience across the population where extent is an expression of the number of potential group members within a particular category, and intensity is an expression of a potential group member's propensity to identify with that category. Intensity of salience will typically be higher among members of ethnic/religious categories than economic/political categories. This is the case because ethnic/religious categoriness is generally more easily recognized than economic/political categoriness, both by members of the category and by those outside the category. Because this is the case, individuals will have their ethnic/religious categoriness reinforced by others more often than they will their economic/political categoriness. As a result of this dual mechanism of internal culturalization and external discrimination, individuals will likely find ethnic/religious categories more salient than economic/political categories. Therefore, potential group members experiencing relative deprivation will more likely respond to appeals to join ethnic/religious rebel movements than economic or political-based ones.

In addition, the existence of indigenous networks varies across categories. ethnic/religious categories typically engender a strong set of indigenous communal networks which encourages the bonding of individuals into collective actors, thus facilitating the formation of guerrilla organizations. On the other hand, indigenous networks within economic/political categories typically do not exist, particularly within the generally underdeveloped and politically repressive Third World, thus inhibiting the formation of strong rebel organizations around those categories. This does not mean that organizations cannot be built from a category of people experiencing economic or political deprivation, only that it will be substantially more difficult.[10]

This observation suggests that ethnic or religious-based separatist groups or nationalist organizations have an inherent advantage over other rebel groups which base their appeals on economic or political categories in mobilizing potential group members into the rebellious fold. The African experience supports this conclusion as most significant nationalist movements in Africa were organized around ethnic divisions rather than political or economic categories. Further, most of the rebel movements one finds when looking at the world in the last 20 years have had an ethnic or religious base: Afghanistan, Cyprus, Ethiopia, the Israeli-occupied West Bank, Lebanon, Peru, and Sri Lanka are all examples.

A second implication is that rebel leaders are faced with a "Catch-22" situation: from a mobilization standpoint, they are likely to have to choose between mobilizing a small percentage of a large number of people (i.e., appealing to economic/political categories), or a larger percentage of a smaller number of people (i.e., appealing to ethnic/religious categories). The significance of this "Catch-22" is found in its ability to address a primary criticism levelled at the relative deprivation model. Wilson (1973: 297) succinctly explains this criticism:

> There is violence at some periods but not at others, and thus explanations based on enduring social conditions ... are not especially helpful—if these conditions were the determinative ones, violence would be more or less continuous.

This criticism suffers from three problems: its proponents fail to appreciate (1) the distinction between absolute and relative deprivation, (2) that different categories have different mobilization potentials, and (3) the impact of the repressive capacity of the state.

The fact that high levels of violent collective action are not observed in all societies that experience high levels of discontent does not demonstrate that the relative deprivation framework is a theoretical bust. First, relative deprivation is subjectively defined by the individual; not all individuals within a society will find "enduring social conditions," which are defined by macro-level theorists, depriving. Therefore, citing absolute levels of deprivation in a society does not adequately address relative deprivation. A second reason that "high" levels of violent collective action are not found in all societies with widespread discontent is because different categories have different mobilization potentials. As discussed above, the existence of societies with "low" levels of civil strife, despite "high" levels of societal stress, is partially a function of the difficulties involved in mobilizing different types of deprivation, rather than in some inherent flaw in the model itself. Thus, we would expect to see less violent collective action in societies where the state represses its citizens across economic or political categories than in societies where discrimination is manifested along ethnic or religious lines. Finally, the state plays a critical role in determining the level and types of violent collective action manifested in society. States that are willing to employ severe repression are likely to entice people to free-ride and sit out collective action regardless of their level of deprivation.

In sum, to this point we have constructed an argument which examines the relationships between rebel groups and individual people who are experiencing deprivation. In doing so we have described a bridge that explains the emergence of collectivities of individuals willing to take up arms against their state: the appeals by groups to relatively deprived individuals facilitates the mobilization of individual deprivation into a rebel organization based on group deprivation. Thus, before participation in armed rebellion is a viable alternative for a given individual, he or she must (1) have some grievance he or she wishes to rectify, (2) feel a sense of corporate identity with other members of a rebel group, (3) identify and hold the state responsible for rectifying his or her grievances, (4) believe that taking up arms is both an acceptable and effective method for addressing those grievances, and (5) join with others in a group which is able to channel collective resources into an armed revolutionary movement. In essence, we have linked the theories of Gurr and Tilly by building a theoretical bridge between the levels of analysis that each addresses. However, to this point, the state has been left out of the analysis. Without incorporating the interaction between the state and rebel groups, our analysis has painted a static picture of the dynamic process of rebellion and revolution. While we have explained how and why individuals enter rebel movements, we have not explicated the process by which these organizations are maintained or changed. In the following section, we consider the state's role in precluding or facilitating the maintenance of rebel movements.

The Interaction of the State and Rebel Groups

While the micro-mobilization process outlined above defines the process by which groups mobilize relatively deprived individuals, it tells us little about the dynamics of the conflict process itself. Thus far we have specified the model of group integration in an environmental vacuum. However, by assuming the existence of a polity in which rebel groups and a state coexist (Tilly 1978), we will uncover the inherent tensions within conflict situations which facilitate and/or inhibit the mobilization of relative deprivation. As McAdam *et. al.* (1988: 716) suggest:

> the SMO must negotiate a niche for itself within the larger organizational environment in which it is embedded. This usually entails the negotiation and management of a complex set of relationships with other organizational actors representing the movement, the state, countermovements, the media, and the general public. How well the SMO manages the contradictory demands imposed by these groups will have a lot to do with the way the movement develops over time.

In other words, it is the interaction between rebel groups and the state over the control of the mobilization process which determines the relative success or failure of insurgency movements.

Internal wars are essentially a process by which states and rebel groups try to maximize their control over the hearts, minds, muscles and wallets of the members of the polity. Both the state and the rebel groups try to maximize the strength of their respective organizations by eliminating the other, as well as by engaging in mutual competition for the mobilization of the masses toward their own side. Tilly (1978) refers to this competition for societal resources as "multiple sovereignty." Integrating Tilly's concept of multiple sovereignty with the model outlined above, the mobilization of relative deprivation requires (1) the appearance of alternative organizations to an existing regime and (2) an acceptance of alternative claims by a significant portion of the population despite the regime's repressive measures (Tilly 1978: 200). In other words, the interaction between rebel groups and the state vying for control of the mobilization of society's resources creates or forecloses opportunities for the formation of political organizations aimed at the violent overthrow of the state.

The decision an individual faces in a multiple sovereignty situation may be modelled as a decision to rebel, protest, remain loyal, or withdraw from politics. To rebel is to actively join the rebel group and take up arms. To protest is to reject the rebellion option, but to press the state to undertake reform. Thus, the protest option represents a decision to remain loyal to the state, but protest some state policies. Finally, loyalty is the decision to remain an active supporter of the state while withdrawal from politics is tantamount to tacit support. The state's ability to generate loyalty, either through coercion, reform, or symbolic appeals to regime legitimacy, will reduce the ability of the rebel group to mobilize a sufficiently large number of people to effectively challenge the state. Even if deprivation is prevalent within a society, and organizations exist ready to mobilize this frustration against the state, the actions of the state may serve as a social control on the rebels' recruitment process.

States may also attempt to channel discontent into protest rather than rebellion. However, the exercise of protest facilitates networks which rebel groups can use to mobilize people. As a result, regimes which face serious challenges have an incentive to eliminate the protest option, forcing discontented individuals to choose between loyalty or withdrawal and the riskier option of rebellion. In fact, we rarely see states expand freedom of speech and press during periods of civil violence. The most recent examples of restriction of the press and public assembly have been witnessed in China and the Israeli-occupied West Bank.

Yet, the tactics used by the state to mobilize loyalty (or discourage protest and rebellion) may, in fact, facilitate rebel recruitment. The use of regime repression, in particular, while having the effect of inhibiting many people from actively joining rebel groups may, ironically, facilitate group entrance by others. According to Tilly (1978), "[r]epression works," but not always. In fact, attempts at repression may release "repression fallout" (Hancock 1975). The reaction by rebel organizations, bystander publics and reference elites to state sponsored violence may actually facilitate movement activity.[11] This scenario implies that state terror tends to facilitate, rather than suppress, the incentive for some people to take up arms against the state.[12] Because the regime identifies a group of people as potential group members, even though they may not be active participants in the rebel group, they may become targets of regime repression. Increasing the threat to the lives of potential group members may substantially reduce the perceived risk of joining the ranks of revolutionary movement (DeNardo 1985: 193). In short, the use of regime repression may alter any individual's calculation about the justification of taking up arms against the state. However, the response of rebellion to acts of state coercion may only hold during the short run. In the long run, if repressive techniques become institutionalized, loyalty and withdrawal, rather than protest or rebellion, will tend to be the rule, contingent upon the state's ability to maintain its monopoly on the use of coercion.

Thus far it has been demonstrated that individuals will exit the regime and enter a rebel group if that group's appeals convince them that they should forego the withdrawal, loyalty or protest options. However, the state's appeals to legitimacy, policies of economic, political, or status redistribution, and/or extremely high levels of institutionalized repression serve as social controls on rebel recruitment. Yet, state-rebel group interaction is not the only source of social control and/or facilitation affecting the mobilization of relative deprivation. As Tilly (1985) suggests, there typically exist several competing rebel movements attempting to mobilize opposition to the state. Where one group is able to absorb smaller groups and form a unified movement, rebel organizations are more likely to mount an effective challenge. Yet, state authorities are aware of this fact and often employ "divide and rule" tactics when faced with rebel challenges.

Therefore, it is theoretically more useful to conceptualize the growth of rebel movements as occurring on two separate, yet interdependent, levels: (1) groups mobilizing individuals, and (2) groups mobilizing other groups. This picture is further complicated by the fact that rebel groups compete with the state and each other in the recruitment process. While the micro-mobilization process explains how there initially comes to exist a confluence of shared interests and organizational strength to challenge the existing state, bloc recruiment (Oberschall 1973: 125) of existing organizations explicates the manner in which these independent organizations may come to form a united front with the resource capacity to effectively pursue armed revolt. In other words, the merger of organizations which have already mobilized individuals to commit resources facilitates the growth of mass movements able to act collectively against the state. This process can be seen in the Nicaraguan revolution. From the early 1970s until July 1978, the FSLN was splintered into three ideologically diverse factions. With each faction pursuing different strategic and tactical goals, the rebel movement posed little threat to Somoza's National Guard. However, with the creation of a general coordinating commission in mid-1978, the tables began to turn. By forming a united front, the FSLN demonstrated for the first time in 18 years that they were capable of launching coordinated attacks in diverse parts of the country and of achieving the occupation of small towns from north to south. These developments in the areas of leadership, organization, and unity signaled the beginning of the end for the Somoza regime.[13]

Despite the benefits to be accrued by rebel groups through bloc recruitment, this process often results in a high level of factionalism, defection and drop-out. Differences in ideological goals, political tactics and organizational structure often result in the loss of members of splinter groups or loyal society. The problem of factionalism plagued the nationalist groups in Zimbabwe's war of national liberation and continues to plague attempts at nation building in post-colonial Zimbabwe.[14]

Synthesizing the socio-psychological and political conflict conceptual frameworks enables us to effectively utilize both the individual and collective levels of analysis, explicate the mobilization process and examine rebel group-state competition. However, this discussion has ignored the fact that modern states enjoy an overwhelming advantage over rebel groups in the realm of coercive capacity. This section has suggested that rebels can challenge states by mobilizing resources and employing them in ways that maximize their capacity *vis-à-vis* the state. Nonetheless, few states lack the coercive capacity necessary to defeat even well-organized rebel forces. The final section builds on Skocpol's (1979) work to suggest that rebel movements are most likely to be successful when the states they are challenging begin to lose a grip on their coercive capacity.

State-Structural Constraints

Gurr (1970) is often criticized for ignoring the critical role of the state in a revolutionary situation. His analysis of state-structural factors is limited to the coercive capacity of the state relative to rebel groups, and probabalistic statements about the resultant magnitude of conflict which is likely to result from different ratios of coercive capacity. In the same manner, Tilly (1978) conceptualizes the state in terms of its resource capacities *vis-à-vis* challenger groups in the polity. While this framework enables him to view rebellion as "politics by other means," it fails to specify how or why rebel groups will be able to militarily challenge the state. Due to these shortcomings, if we accept the analysis outlined in the previous sections, then we must answer why it is that rebellions and revolutions are such rare events. According to the model sketched above, groups merely need to issue persuasive appeals and they will be in a position to militarily challenge the state. Yet, without the opening of political opportunities, either through the breakdown of the state's repressive apparatus or the infusion of international aid to the rebel movement, regardless of the number of appeals issued in a society, states are rarely overthrown from below. Not only must rebel organizations be able to mobilize resources, they must also have the opportunity to employ them. Thus, only to the extent that political opportunities exist will rebel groups be able to make full use of their coercive capabilities. In the case of rebellion, the relevant political opportunity is the breakdown of a state's coercive capacity. Given that states enjoy a virtual monopoly on the coercive capacity within society, that breakdown can only be sufficiently explained by employing a framework that elaborates the state's relations with non-state actors.

The implicit assumption that rebel groups can challenge states is one of the fundamental faults that Skocpol (1979) finds with the "voluntarist" schools of thought. Taking a structural perspective, she emphatically rejects the voluntarist position that revolutions can be explained in terms of the deliberate actions or strategies of revolutionary organizations or the state. Revolutions, for structuralists such as Skocpol, cannot be orchestrated, they simply come.

While we believe that Skocpol's structural analysis imparts new insights to understanding the nature of revolution, we do not believe that it is a paradigmatic panacea. In fact, by itself, we find her analysis to be theoretically incomplete. From her perspective, the revolutionary potential of the masses, along with the organizational structure of these movements, are taken as theoretical givens. However, by "assuming away" the explanatory potential of the strategic tactics of rebellious organizations and the state, Skocpol's structural framework turns out to be a house of cards. It is her position that having constructed a structural theory of revolution, absent of any voluntarist infuences, she has proven that nonvoluntarist theories can provide both the necessary and sufficient conditions for revolution. Yet, simply choosing to ignore the "voluntarist" variables does not refute their potential explanatory power. Regardless of the degree of explanatory power that Skocpol's structural model possesses, she gives us no *prima facie* reason to reject the use of voluntarist theories all together. While the structural relationship between the state and rebel organizations is of fundamental importance in explaining the dynamics of revolutions, these societal arrangements are not created independently of the strategies employed in the formation of challenger movements, and calculated state responses.

Skocpol (1979) sheds some light on the issue of how rebel groups are able to militarily challenge a state by suggesting that strong states are relatively unassailable by rebel groups. Casting her theory in a more deterministic mold than we find necessary, she nevertheless reminds us that states are constrained by their structural relations with dominant classes and their competition with other states in the international system. Not all states are able to retain their strength when confronted by the competing claims of their responsibilities to dominant classes and their own interests in the international system. She suggests that revolutions are only possible when states effectively collapse as a result of their inability to balance these competing claims on their resources.

Skocpol's main insight is that states are semi-autonomous entities *vis-à-vis* powerful non-state actors within the society: they are not completely penetrated by dominant classes (*à la* Marxism), nor are they merely forums for the competition of interest groups (*à la* pluralism). Instead, a state's power *vis-à-vis* the society it governs is only partially a function of its relations with the various powerful actors within that society, as well as its relations with other states in the international system. In other words, state power is a function of the state's structural positions in society and the international system. This is an important insight because it provides the clue to the potential causes of a state's fall from power and the ability of rebel groups to militarily challenge the state; precisely the insights that are missing in Gurr (1970) and Tilly (1978).

Her analysis of the importance of dominant classes to state power is similar to Tilly's discussion of the state's reliance on polity members (i.e., powerful groups within society). The crucial distinction is that Skocpol defines these groups as class actors whereas Tilly leaves open the possibility that non-class based groups may be relevant in certain societies. Because of the greater flexibility that Tilly's analysis allows us, we prefer to discuss the importance of powerful groups as opposed to dominant classes. Nevertheless, while Tilly suggests that a polity member's shift in support from the state to a challenger group will undermine the state's ability to crush popular support, he fails to specify how or why such a shift would take place. One of Skocpol's main achievements is that she provides answers to those questions by outlining two ways in which a state's ability to crush rebel groups may become undermined: withdrawal of support from dominant classes and foreign competition.

Drawing on the social revolutions which took place in France, Russia and China she shows that the withdrawal of support of the landed aristocracy and/or the military led to the collapse of each of these states. In each case, foreign competition—particularly the involvement in costly wars—led the state to attempt to increase its extractive capacity *vis-à-vis* the powerful groups in each society. It was resistance to the state's claim on greater levels of societal resources (to use Tilly's terminology) that led these groups to withdraw their support from the state. Because the state needed this support, its withdrawal led to the state's collapse.

In what ways can we draw on Skocpol's analysis to complete the model we have been constructing? First, we must note that the state, powerful as it is, is not omnipotent: it must have some degree of support from powerful non-state members of society. In many Third World nations these often include representatives of domestic and international capital and the military. Without the support of both of these groups, the state will be unable to quell popular unrest and will probably become the victim of a coup d'etat. Second, states must be wary of the designs of other states in the international system. Both the United States and the Soviet Union, as well as other powerful states, engage in de-stabilization activities as a routine part of their covert foreign policies. Thus, states, particularly those in the Third World, have several interests they must consider aside from their own. Yet, the fact remains that states do not fall on a routine basis. More importantly, few fall as a result of a successfully prosecuted revolutionary war. Thus, the prognosis for rebel groups is not terribly promising.

To some, the analysis in this section may appear to render our previous discussion useless. For, if only powerful groups (i.e., not rebel groups) and international crises can break down a state's coercive capacity, then what is the point of studying individuals, groups and micro-mobilization? The individual and collective levels of analysis are important for at least two reasons: (1) rebel groups can play a role in bringing the withdrawal of support of key groups, or the the power of other actors in the international system, to bear on state power, and (2) when a political opportunity (i.e., a decline in state power) occurs, we need theoretical guidance for understanding how and why groups are, or are not, able to take advantage of the moment. Groups like the ANC and PLO are aware of the importance of international pressure to help weaken the states they are challenging and have sophisticated public relations wings which carry on this part of the struggle. Further, rebel groups often attack economic targets such as energy depots and other industrial installations. By undermining the economic structure of the state, they hope to weaken its coercive capacity. Thus, rebel groups can play a role in diminishing state power by lobbying the international community to levy economic and political sanctions against it, attempting to undermine the economy domestically, undermining public confidence with campaigns of terror, and raising the costs of maintaining the state by attacking it militarily.

In sum, while rebel groups must issue appeals in an effort to mobilize guerrillas, few people are likely to eschew the free-rider option unless they perceive that the rebellion has some chance of success. While one of the types of appeal that we identified above is appeal to the utilitarian value of rebellion, people are not stupid, and when the state enjoys the support of powerful domestic groups and is not entangled in international crises, its overwhelming coercive capacity is likely to convince people that rebellion is not likely to be successful, regardless of the arguments they hear to the contrary. Therefore, while we cannot accept that groups and leaders have no impact upon the genesis of rebellion, we recognize that people are not free to challenge states simply because they want to. Instead, rebellions and revolutions are an extremely complicated outcome of the intersection of people's actions at all three levels of analysis: the individual, the collective and the social-structural levels.

Conclusion

This article has presented a synthesis of three conceptual frameworks: the socio-psychological, political conflict, and structural-determinist. This synthesis is based on a recognition of the importance of the three levels of analysis presented above:- the individual, collective, and social-structural levels. Now the important question is: How can we assess this synthesis? In other words, What hypotheses does it yield? It is our conclusion that by incorporating all three levels of analysis, our model introduces some new hypotheses not found in previous work. In addition, because it is a synthetic model, it incorporates many of the arguments found in Gurr (1970), Tilly (1978), and Skocpol (1979).

In conjunction with Gurr's analysis we propose that relative deprivation is a necessary condition for the outbreak of rebellion. In addition, the model suggests that before individuals will join a rebellion, they must be exposed to appeals to (1) the corporate identity of the group, (2) relative deprivation, (3) the identification of the state as responsible, (4) normative justifications for, and (5) the utilitarian value of, armed revolt. Further, we extend Gurr's analysis by elucidating not only the individual's receptivity to appeals, but the group's role in issuing those appeals and channelling collective discontent into positive action.

Borrowing from Tilly (1978), the model posits that resource mobilization is a necessary condition for the manifestations of revolutionary challenges to state power. In addition, the model proposes that both developed networks and salient categories must either exist or be constructed by the rebel groups. We build on Tilly's analysis with the hypothesis that appeals to fraternalistic relative deprivation enhance the mobilization of monetary resources, but appeals to individual relative deprivation will enhance the mobilization of human resources.

Further, relying on Skocpol (1979), the model posits that rebel groups are more likely to mount effective challenges when the state is weakened by its inability to balance its own interests with powerful groups within the society it governs, or other actors in the international system. Thus, while deprivation and mobilization are necessary conditions, they are not sufficient: the state must experience some significant crisis before the political opportunity exists for rebel groups to effectively challenge the state. However, unlike Skocpol, we suggest that rebel groups can play an active role in bringing both international and domestic pressure to bear on the state they are assailing.

Finally, our model suggests two hypotheses which have not been suggested in the literature. First, appeals must psychologically connect individuals with a larger category of people experiencing similar types and/or levels of deprivation before they can take advantage of their collective strength. Second, the model suggests that the translation of individual into fraternalistic relative deprivation is a necessary condition for armed revolt.

To the extent that these hypotheses can be operationalized, they can be subjected to statistical analyses and empirical falsification. However, we are unaware of any standard data sets which would enable one to operationalize the concepts discussed. Individual level data is not available for any historical rebellion that we know of. Therefore, we are left with two options for examining the empirical utility of the model. The first is thick descriptive case studies. While a multitude of such studies exist for several cases, few of them try to theoretically incorporate the three levels of analysis we have identified. Of course, the model we have developed here is not the only way to theoretically incorporate these three levels of analysis. Rather than suggest that others should explicitly utilize this model, we merely call for those doing thick descriptive case studies to theoretically specify the relevant variables at the individual, collective, and social-structural levels when performing their analyses.

The second approach to examining the empirical utility of this model is one which has only recently begun to receive attention in the literature. Seventeen years ago Gurr (1972: 44) commented that "at some point in the near future ... computer simulations of civil conflict processes should be possible." Lee (1987), Richardson (1987), and Marwell et al. (1988) are examples of computer simulations which study some of the processes examined above. Computer simulations allow us to verify that our models are logically consistent, and they give us a laboratory where we can hold variables constant and determine the impact of changes in other variables. Of course, before we can discuss "real cases" we must collect data from actual cases. However, those who wish to perform simulations of specific cases have a wealth of descriptive studies from which to code and compile data. Utilizing these resources will allow those of us who don't have a "knack" for history to begin to perform meaningful studies of social conflict processes which examine human interaction in real cases over time.

In conclusion, we recognize the value of aesthetically pleasing, parsimonious theories. Yet, within each of the three conceptual frameworks we have identified areas where the theoriests can learn from each other. Further, we contend that we are more likely to gain a better understanding of rebellion if we begin to synthesize across levels of analysis rather than debate the relative merits of the theories in each camp. We offer this model as a first step in that direction.

NOTES

1 Categorizing theories into broad groups is a necessarily reductionist task; no individual theory may be justly treated in such an exercise. Nonetheless, the categorization is heuristic in that it gives us a starting point from which we can approach a synthesis.

2 Examples of the socio-psychological approach to the study of rebellion and revolution include Davies (1962), Smelser (1962), Geschwender (1964), Gurr (1970) and Popkin (1979).

3 Oberschall (1973), Gamson (1975), McCarthy and Zald (1977), Tilly (1978) and McAdam (1982) are examples of the political conflict approach.

4 The structural-determinist approach is represented by scholars such as Moore (1966), Wolf (1969), Paige (1975), Trimberger (1978) and Skocpol (1979).

5 For a review of the theoretical literature, see Taylor (1984). Zimmermann (1983) reviews the empirical literature.

6 We are only concerned with organizations which enjoy the active participation of their members, as opposed to professional social movement organizations (McCarthy & Zald 1973), which do not receive the active participation of their members.

7 For a discussion of these issues and events see Martin & Johnson (1981: 73-91), Cilliers (1985: 218-223), Lan (1985), and Ranger (1985: 177-222).

8 Snow et. al. (1986) use the term "frame alignment."

9 In this analysis, class-based deprivation is subsumed under the latter category.

10 McCarthy and Zald (1977: 1218) argue that "[s]ocial movements whose related populations are highly organized internally ... are more likely than are others to spawn organized forms."

11 See Gurr (1972), Hibbs (1973), Lichbach and Gurr (1981), and Muller and Seligson (1987).

12 For a discussion of the differential impacts repression can have on violent collective action, see Lichbach (1987).

13 For a review of these events see Booth (1982).

14 For a review of the problem of ethnic factionalism, see Sithole (1980).

The Social Origins of Dictatorship, Democracy and Socialist Revolution in Central America*

JEFFERY M. PAIGE**

ABSTRACT

Barrington Moore Jr.'s *Social Origins of Dictatorship and Democracy* remains the most widely accepted and influential theory not only of revolution but of the origins of democracy, authoritarianism and revolutionary socialism. But the political histories of El Salvador, Costa Rica and Nicaragua, three small countries in a backward peripheral region, tend to refute all of the major tenets of Moore's model. The Central American bourgeoisie did not support democratic revolution but were more likely to back authoritarianism. Bourgeois support for even limited democracy was highly contingent and related to the absence of serious challenge from below. Imperial control, not traditional agrarian bureaucracy, critically weakened the bourgeoisie and opened the way for socialist revolution, and these revolutions were a result of capitalist pulverization of the peasantry, not the persistence of cohesive peasant villages. Moore's model dramatically underestimates the influence of imperial controls in weakening traditional ruling classes and the role of workers and intellectuals in expanding the scope of human freedom not only in Central America but in the Third World generally.

WE ARE ALL STUDENTS OF Barrington Moore, Jr., not only those of us like Theda Skocpol and Charles Tilly, who had the privilege of studying directly with him, or like Jack Goldstone and Jeff Goodwin, with one of his students (in this case Theda Skocpol), but also like Victoria Bonnell, Susan Eckstein or myself who have been profoundly influenced by his work. It would be fair to say that Barrington Moore, Jr. created the modern study of revolution just as he contributed profoundly to the current golden age of comparative historical sociology and the revival of political sociology. In this year of anniversaries of revolutions great and small, the French, the Chinese, Cuban, the Nicaraguan, it is only fitting that we turn to an examination of the ideas of a man who restored the study of revolution to a central place at the core of the sociological discipline. His *Social Origins of Dictatorship and Democracy* remains the most widely accepted and influential theory not only of revolution but of the origins of democracy, authoritarianism and revolutionary socialism.

El Salvador, Costa Rica and Nicaragua, three small countries in a region that was once the most obscure corner of the Spanish colonial empire, may seem a strange place to begin an evaluation of a theory based on studies of the

* This paper was presented at the Annual Meeting of the American Sociological Association, San Francisco, California, August 8, 1989.
** Department of Sociology, University of Michigan, Ann Arbor, Michigan, U.S.A. 48109-1382.

great revolutions, the French, the Chinese, and implicitly but fundamentally, the Russian. Indeed Moore himself (1966, xiii) cautions against the study of small countries since "the decisive causes of their politics lie outside their boundaries," although he acknowledges a certain discomfort at bypassing some worthy, if diminutive, revolutions in such obscure places as the Korean peninsula, Cuba and Indochina. But the cases of Costa Rica, El Salvador and Nicaragua present us with a fortuitous natural experiment in the study of revolutions since they contain within themselves Moore's three routes into the modern political world—democracy, authoritarianism and revolutionary socialism.

Indeed, it would be difficult to find three political systems anywhere in the world that differ among themselves as much as do contemporary Costa Rica, El Salvador and Nicaragua. Costa Rica has the longest lived democracy in Latin America. Since 1889, when it held the first fully free election in Latin America, Costa Rica has, with the exception of two brief periods in 1917-1919 and 1948, operated as a democracy. Since 1948, Costa Rica has been the only country in Latin America to continuously hold free elections contested by more than one political party. In 1986, Oscar Arias Sanchez was elected president after defeating his party's chosen candidate in a contested primary as well as winning the subsequent free election. El Salvador, by contrast, suffered under what is, arguably, the longest lived military dictatorship in Latin America from 1932 to 1979, and the military still holds a dominant position in spite of nominally contested elections in 1984 and 1989. On June 1 of 1989 Alfredo Cristiani of the National Republican Alliance (ARENA) party, widely described as neo-fascist by its opponents, assumed office as president of El Salvador. While professing democracy, Cristiani failed to distance himself from party founder and admirer of Adolf Hitler, Roberto D'Aubuisson. Nicaragua is one of only two surviving socialist states in the Western Hemisphere and the only one on the continental mainland. The slogan of the seventh anniversary of its revolution in 1986 could stand for the tenth as well—"the greatest triumph is to have survived." Democracy, neo-fascism and revolutionary socialism, Moore's three paths, are all present in contemporary Central America.

Furthermore, the three countries share a number of historical and structural similarities including a common isthmian location, a common history of foreign domination and a common origin in the same province of the Spanish colonial empire. All are small, peripheral agricultural export economies dependent on one or two primary commodities, and in all three one commodity, coffee, has been the major source of wealth, foreign exchange, government revenue and political power from the mid-nineteenth century to the present. In all three countries an agrarian elite of coffee growers, processors and exporters ruled almost without interruption until the second half of the twentieth century and, to a greater or lesser degree, control the fate of these nations to this day. The capitalist transformation of agriculture which figures so prominently in Moore's theory came to Central America with the nineteenth-century coffee trade. Despite all of these similarities both the behavior of these coffee elites and the political systems they shaped could not have been more divergent.

What accounts for this divergence? In *Social Origins* Moore argues that democracy is a product of an assault by an insurgent bourgeoisie on a backward landed aristocracy ("no bourgeoisie, no democracy" [1966: 414]), that authoritarian "fascist" regimes result from a coalition between a dominant landed aristocracy and a weak bourgeoisie, and that socialist revolution occurs when a mass revolt of cohesive peasant villages overwhelms a strong landed elite and a weak bourgeoisie constrained by a powerful agrarian state. None of these things, however, is true of the social origins of dictatorship, democracy or socialist revolution in Central America.

First, in none of these countries is there a collison between an industrial bourgeoisie and a landed class. In all three cases an agrarian bourgeoisie of coffee producers combined land owning and industrial functions in a single class, and this pattern is in fact common throughout Latin America (Frank, 1969: 399; Stavenhagen, 1968: 2; Zeitlin and Ratcliff, 1988: 181-192). Peripheral capitalism provides few opportunities for the development of an autonomous bourgeoisie, strong or weak, based on manufacturing for internal markets. Instead, in Central America, the demands of the world economy created a capitalist transformation based on the export of a primary agricultural commodity to the developed world. Traditional land owners, enterprising foreign immigrants, colonial and republican officials all rushed to acquire land and make themselves into capitalists, confounding the distinction between the two forms of property (Browning, 1971: 169; Stone, 1982: 40; Wheelock, 1980: 17). Furthermore, the production of coffee itself created a technical division between cultivation or production proper and industrial processing of the harvested crop. Processors are industrial capitalists using an agricultural raw material while cultivators are land owners in labor intensive agriculture. The distinction between the two factions does create divisions within Central American elites but the two factions are linked by function, finance, ownership and kinship into a single class (Dunkerly, 1982: 54; Torres-Rivas, 1978: 44-45; Winson, 1981: 281-285). The ruling classes of Central America are neither backward agrarians nor an industrial bourgeoisie. They are instead an agrarian bourgeoisie. The closest historical parallels are Moore's modernizing English landlords.

Where this agrarian bourgeoisie of coffee producers and processors had most fully transformed itself into a capitalist class, in El Salvador, the result was not democracy but authoritarianism and neo-fascism. The Salvadoran agrarian bourgeoisie created the single most efficient coffee production system in the world and did so on a fully capitalist basis, employing wage labor which, by the 1920s, had already begun to lose most of its remaining ties to the land. Extra-economic coercion, used extensively in coffee cultivation in neighboring Guatemala, was unnecessary in El Salvador because nineteenth-century land expropriations had created a large reserve army of landless, migratory coffee pickers who were politically repressed but paid wages (Baloyra, 1982: 25-27; Menjivar, 1980: 142-143; Paige, 1987; White, 1973: 118-119). The economically backward Junker allies of German fascism are nowhere to be found in El Salvador. Yet it was precisely these progressive agrarian capitalists that supported the bloodiest repression in the region's history during the *matanza* (massacre) of 1932 and unflinchingly backed a repressive military dictatorship for almost fifty years. They did so not because they needed servile labor to survive in a world market but because they needed repression to put down a militant, organized proletariat. It was not labor repressive agriculture that drove the Salvadorans to neofascism but rather revolutionary socialism. The Salvadoran case raises the possibility that a bourgeoisie, agrarian or industrial, supports democracy only when it is not faced with a revolutionary challenge from below.

Democracy in Costa Rica did not come into being as a result of a "bourgeois revolution," since the agrarian bourgeoisie backed counterrevolution, but rather through the actions of middle class intellectuals, workers and small farmers. The Costa Rican bourgeoisie, which had lost much of its control over the land and become an elite of industrial coffee processors, supported only limited "bourgeois" democracy which they controlled through paternalism and outright fraud (Cardoso, 1977: 192-193; Stone, 1982: 215-237). When they were faced with a militant communist-led working class that threatened their control they too turned to armed counterrevolution and backed José Figueres' 1948 anti-Communist revolt. To their surprise and dismay Figueres and his middle class intellectual supporters came to terms with their working class opponents, enlisted the support of the urban middle classes and enterprising small farmers, and relegated their erstwhile allies to a political obscurity where they have languished for more than forty years (Ameringer, 1978: 69-70; Stone, 1982: 313-314; Winson, 1981: 135-136). Costa Rican democracy is based on the middle class intellectuals and small farmers who have been its principal beneficiaries. It was established by revolutionary workers who achieved substantial although more limited benefits. Fortunately, an unarmed bourgeoisie was unable to prevent these developments.

Democracy was in fact the ideology of the backward land owners of Nicaragua, not the progressive capitalists of El Salvador or the agro-industrialists of Costa Rica, and in the end their actions contributed to a socialist, not a democratic revolution, based on a revolt of the urban poor, not the peasantry. Weakened by United States intervention, civil war and the Somoza dynasty, the landowners of Nicaragua never succeeded in carrying out a capitalist transformation, agrarian or industrial, and remained in 1979 the most backward and least capitalist of the three coffee elites (Biderman, 1983: 12; Deere and Marchetti, 1981: 44; Wheelock, 1980: 42-44). Their support for democracy came not as a result of a successful capitalist challenge but rather from arrested capitalist development. It was based on opposition to the corruption and tyranny of the Somozas' personal dictatorship (Gilbert, 1985; 1988: 105-127; Paige, 1989; Vilas, 1986: 132). In Nicaragua, democracy became a tool to advance the interests of a frustrated bourgeoisie, while in El Salvador, by contrast, it became, after 1932, an impediment to continued bourgeois hegemony. No peasant revolt broke out in Nicaragua because by 1979 there was little or no traditional peasantry left to revolt. It was not the backward-looking, traditional peasant communities which provided the dynamite that exploded the old order, but rather the floating informal proletariat of country and city created by the capitalist transformation of agriculture (Lopez et al., 1980: 185-186; Vilas, 1986: 118-119). Capitalism, not peasant communitarianism, once more proved to be revolutionary.

How could Moore have gone so wrong? Are there any general lessons that can be learned from these startling exceptions to Moore's thesis? It seems apparent that Moore's decision to ignore peripheral cases of which he knew little was not sound methodology. Central American revolutions are not caused by powerful countries "outside their boundaries." The United States, for example, has had remarkably little success in influencing them despite concerted and expensive efforts to do so. But there are also deeper problems that go to the heart of Moore's argument. First, as analysts to European historical developments have argued, the bourgeoisie has seldom played the decisive role in the development of full parliamentary democracy based on universal suffrage (Blackbourn and Eley, 1984; Stephens, 1989; Therborn, 1977). Instead other classes, including in Central America workers, intellectuals, small farmers, and even repressed land owners, have made a contribution to its development. What the Central American bourgeoisie wanted was a limited or bourgeois democracy as in Costa Rica. The concept of a "bourgeois revolution" leading automatically to parliamentary democracy may finally be ready for decent burial by Marxist and non-Marxist alike.

Second, bourgeois support for even limited or bourgeois democracy is highly contingent on and related to the absence of a challenge from below. The El Salvadoran elite in 1932 faced the only mass Communist insurrection in the history of Latin America. It is impossible to understand their ferocious authoritarianism without an appreciation of this event. A bourgeoisie, agrarian or industrial, under revolutionary pressure may be just as dangerous to human freedom as a backwardlanded aristocracy.

Third, the triumph of revolutionary socialism is closely tied to the advance of imperialism. The weak, backward, agrarian bourgeoisie of Nicaragua was not a consequence of a powerful agrarian bureaucracy, either colonial Spanish or Mesoamerican, but rather of imperial controls imposed by the United States. Similar imperial controls leading to a similarly weakened and frustrated bourgeoisie were critical to the success of both the Cuban and the Vietnamese revolutions (Lieberman, 1989; Williams, 1966: 191-192).

Fourth, socialist revolution is a consequence of capitalist pulverization of the peasantry, not a persistence of communitarian patterns. In this latter contention Moore might have been misled by the Russian case that he knew so well. The capitalist transformation of the peasantry was as important to the success of the Cuban and Vietnamese revolutions as it was to the Nicaraguan

(Lieberman, 1989; MacEwan, 1985: 421-422; Paige, 1975: 333). In short, the socialist transformation of the periphery is a result of the capitalist incorporation of these areas under imperial control, not of the persistence of backward social formations. Socialism is not the last gasp of dying social classes but the desperate hope of new classes generated in the capitalist periphery.

For Moore, socialist revolution was the unintended consequence of actions by backward-looking classes that led only to dictatorship—hence the facile contrast between democracy and the equivalent dictatorship of fascism and communism in the title of *Social Origins*. If there is a hero in Moore's book it is the modernizing, industrial bourgeoisie of the imperial United States at mid-century, defending democracy against the heirs of backward agrarian orders in the parallel dictatorships of fascism and communism. But in Central America the agrarian bourgeoisie, aided by this triumphant bourgeoisie, has violently opposed democracy in El Salvador, reluctantly supported it in Costa Rica, and even desperately fought for it in Nicaragua. In Central America more reliable allies in the search for human freedom have been found among yeoman farmers, militant workers and middle class intellectuals. A triumphant bourgeoisie has, since Immanuel Wallerstein's long sixteenth century, transformed the world, but not necessarily in directions of its own choosing. The expansion of the scope of human freedom, first in the great democratic revolutions of the eighteenth century and now in the great socialist transformations of the twentieth, we owe not to this all-conquering bourgeoisie but rather to farmers and artisans, factory workers and students, poets and journalists, ordinary men and ordinary women who sought human dignity in the future, not mechanical solidarity in the past. It is they who are the true heroes and the true heroines of revolutions great and small.

Class, Dependency and Revolution in the Caribbean: Preliminary Considerations for a Comparative Study of Aborted and Successful Revolutions

JOSÉ A. MORENO*

ABSTRACT

This paper is an attempt to demonstrate that social revolutions in the Caribbean may best be understood and explained if a dependency theory framework is used. The paper argues that the small countries of the Caribbean, because of their size, geographic position, scarcity of natural resources and other demographic factors have been dependent first on the colonial powers and later on the industrialized nations for a longer period of time and in greater depth than most other Latin American countries.

The paper seeks to demonstrate that a successful revolutionary process in the Caribbean must meet the challenge of internally restructuring the class structure of the society while at the same time breaking economic and political ties that made it dependent on the colonial or industrial centers. It further contends that the external ties of dependency reinforce and perpetuate the previously existing class structure and that unless such ties are eliminated, the internal restructuring of the society cannot be accomplished.

THIS ESSAY ARGUES THAT SOCIAL structure and social change in the Caribbean may best be understood if studied in historical perspective and with a framework of dependency theory (Chilcote and Edelstein 1986; Petras 1983: 1-71). Few areas of the world have experienced such a long-lasting and all-encompassing history of colonial and imperialist domination. From the time of the first settlements by Christopher Columbus in Santo Domingo to the present, natural and human resources of the area have been exploited in the interest of outsiders, with few benefits, beyond survival, accruing to the peoples of the region (Knight 1978; Williams 1970; Pierre 1981).

Colonial situations are typically characterized by a dominant power with military and political control over another nation whose human and economic resources are systematically drained and funneled to meet certain needs of the metropolis (Cesaire 1972). In many cases, however, the dominated nations succeed in counteracting foreign encroachment with various strategies of conflict and adaptation that allow them to survive culturally and

* Department of Sociology, University of Pittsburgh, Pennsylvania, 15260, U.S.A.

politically. This was not the case in the Caribbean. After the native Indian population was decimated through open war or through the hardships of slave labor, what was left in the Caribbean was an aggregate of peoples uprooted from Europe, Africa, and later from Asia, without any purpose in common but the imposed obligation to work and produce for the benefit of the metropolis (Williams 1966; Riverand 1972).

The cultures and new societies that emerged in the Caribbean through the work and toil of the succeeding generations bore the imprint of their origins in dependence and colonialism. In other words, dependence and colonialism were not patterns of behavior imposed temporarily from outside. In the emergent nations of the Caribbean such patterns of behavior were rooted in the formation of the societies, in their mode of production, in their culture, their form of social organization, and in their very raison d'être. Not even the new nations of Asia and Africa, subject to colonial domination until the second half of the twentieth century, were so completely permeated by patterns of cultural and social dependence as the nations of the Caribbean. In the emergence of Caribbean societies, the relations of dependence on the metropolis determined, the mode of production, from the encomienda, slavery and plantation economies of the past, to the one-crop export economies of the present. Dependence also dictated the forms of political organization and types of rulers from governors, caudillos and dictators to military juntas and subservient civilian regimes. One could argue that all forms of cultural and social life in Caribbean societies have been directly or indirectly conditioned by such relations of dependence (Blassingame 1979). It would not be hard for social historians to demonstrate that dependence on the metropolis determined the ethnicity, population composition, geographic distribution, patterns of migration, family organization, stratification systems and the occupational structures of Caribbean societies. One could also argue that other basic institutions such as the legal system, religion and education were also molded within a cultural framework of values and beliefs that were supportive of the systems' of domination.

The Caribbean islands were the first colonial territories in the Americas. Because of their geographic location, they were coveted by the European metropolis for commercial and strategic reasons. The islands were the ports of calls for the Spanish galleons with their shipments of gold and silver and for the English pirates, French buccaneers and Dutch filibusters who preyed on them (Knight 1978: 148). Throughout the nineteenth century, European nations and the United States competed with each other over the possession, ownership and domination of the islands (Guerra 1975). Most islands—and their inhabitants—were at one time or other purchased, bartered, exchanged, invaded, traded or given away as compensation for war losses.

Throughout the nineteenth century, various wars of liberation attempted to bring about political independence to Haiti, Cuba and the Dominican Republic. Puerto Rico was handed over by Spain to the United States to compensate for the war losses of the latter in the Spanish-American war (Thomas

1971). From the time these countries gained their political independence, their predominantly export economies became increasingly dependent on trade with the United States. As Spanish nationals, bureaucrats, military officers, importers and land owners left to return to Spain, American investors stepped in with their occupation forces to take over the land and other sources of production in Cuba and Puerto Rico (Riverand 1972: 218-235). By the turn of the century, Cuba had gained limited political independence within the framework of the Platt amendment, and Puerto Rico was traded over from one colonial power to another (Guerra 1974; Leuchsering 1973: 57-87). By the middle 1920s both countries were more economically dependent on the U.S. than they ever were on Spain (López 1973).

With political independence each of the new nations soon became an arena for social and political conflicts, struggle for power among competing elites, interest groups and emerging new classes. The immediate result was often economic stagnation and fiscal bankruptcy, political disintegration and general social disorganization (Yglesias 1980: 48-117). North American interests made further inroads into the local economies often protected by the military power of the ever-present marines and always supported by the various "protectionist" policies of the American government. When the struggle for power among classes or local elites began to interfere with the development of American interests, American troops were dispatched, dictators were established or military juntas were encouraged to restore conditions of stability. Thus, we have throughout the Caribbean, from the beginning of the twentieth century, a succession of American military interventions followed by long periods of dictatorships with only a sprinkling of shortlived experiments in democracy (Cassá 1984: 73-93). It is in this historical context and using a perspective of dependency theory that I intend to study the concept of revolution and its applicability to events that have taken place in the Caribbean. First of all, by revolution I understand a drastic process of change that profoundly affects the economic foundations, the institutional structure and the social organization of a society resulting in a reconstitution of the social order and in a new culture (Wallace 1956). The immediate consequences of such a profound process of change would be a reorganization of production and a redefinition of the class relations emerging from it.

It becomes apparent that a process with such far-reaching consequences as the one described above has not often taken place in the Caribbean. Although the Caribbean nations were a theater for an unending series of revolts, coups, rebellions and uprisings after the wars of independence, it is clear that very few of these events produced any drastic reorganization of society by altering relations of production and class alignment. Most of these coups and rebellions were engineered to substitute power holders or at best to bring about limited political participation and economic benefits to segments of the elite hitherto excluded from such rewards. Few of these benefits, if any, trickled down to the peasants, the unemployed and to the dispossessed masses in general. Circulation of elites, either through dictators and military juntas or through elected presidents, provided institutional mechanisms to maintain the same relations of production and the same class structure (Nun 1968).

The only exceptions to this generalization, although vastly different in their accomplishments, were the Haitian revolution of 1804 and the Cuban revolution of 1959. It is not the purpose of this paper to undertake the task of comparing these two revolutionary processes. Although there are some evident similarities: an economically prosperous colony attempts to break away from a situation of dependence by fighting an all too powerful metropolis (France 1804, United States 1959) and by tearing down a given set of relations of production, (plantation slavery in 1804 and dependent capitalism in 1959) the cultural and historical differences separating the two cases are such that it seems acceptable for this paper to present only a preliminary description of each case separately while showing how each of the cases qualifies as a revolution.

1. Class and Revolution in Haiti: 1790-1804

The events that took place in Haiti from 1790 to 1804 could be considered as stages in a revolutionary process that sought to break loose from the political and economic domination of France. In this sense, the Haitian revolution is not different from the wars of independence of either the United States or other Latin American countries. What makes the Haitian war of independence unique are other facts and events that were not present in most other wars of independence and that provided the Haitian war of independence with the social characteristics of a true revolutionary process. The Haitian revolution not only brought about political independence from the metropolis, but it totally crushed an oppressive class system establishing new relations of production and attempting to restructure a new social order (James 1963; Ott 1973; Manigat 1972).

The class structure of Haitian society in the XVIIth century had been molded by a metropolis that had burst into a dramatic revolution in 1789. Resembling the ancien regime in France, Haitian society was made up of a tiny white upper class composed mostly of wealthy planters, high ranking government officials and military officers (James 1963: 27-62; Ott 1973: 3-27). The members of this class identified themselves with the prosperous entrepreneurial upper bourgeoisie in France where many of them lived after acquiring wealth in the colony. Some of them lived in the colony surrounded by mulatto servants and black slaves. There was also a small group of white merchants, craftsmen, shopkeepers, small land holders and government bureaucrats that could be classified as a petit bourgeoisie. They lived mostly in the capital city and in some other provincial towns. While the upper bourgeoisie identified itself almost totally with the metropolis, the children of the petit bourgeoisie began to emerge as a creole society, although its cultural patterns were reflections of those in the metropolis. The petit bourgeoisie emulated and competed for the status and privileges of the upper bourgeoisie.

Next to the petit bourgeoisie, but quite distant in terms of status, was an underclass of mulatto and black freedmen who had obtained their freedom through money and services or through the generosity of some white slaveowners. Some of these mulattoes were the illegitimate children of white colonists or had rendered extraordinary services to the white planters either as servants, concubines, nannies or foremen in the plantations (Hall 1971: 187-226). Finally, at the bottom of the social structure was a mass of black slaves brought in from Africa or born in the colony. While the white colonial and creole population numbered scarcely 30,000, the black slaves numbered about 500,000. They made up the labor force in the plantations, worked as servants for their masters and lived in the most abject and unsanitary conditions. From the point of view of the metropolis and of the white colonists, Haiti was an ideal colony. It provided the emergent French capitalist bourgeoisie with highly valued commodities such as sugar, coffee, tobacco, indigo and hides. For Bordeau, Marseilles and Nantes trade and commerce with the colony was heavier than with any other part of the world. Haiti was considered the most prosperous and profitable colony in the western hemisphere (James 1963: 45-57).

The revolutionary process was unwittingly triggered by a revolt of the white plantation and slave owners who in 1790 demanded representation in the Estates General in Paris. This group of wealthy planters from the most prosperous colony in the western hemisphere demanded the rights of equality and representation only for themselves (Ott 1973: 28-46). Soon their claims were echoed by members of the small white petit bourgeoisie of the colony. In order to strengthen its position, the upper bourgeoisie sought and obtained for a time the support of the free mulatto and black population in the island. The white petit bourgeoisie resented the encroachment of its rights by the metropolitan bureaucracy and the higher status of the wealthy planters now allied with the free blacks and mulattoes. But the white petit bourgeoisie particularly opposed the idea of the free blacks and mulattoes enjoying privileges hitherto reserved to the whites (Logan 1968: 88-89).

For the first three years the two factions of the white bourgeoisie fought against each other with the help of the black and mulatto freedmen and of the slaves. Each faction fought to maintain its privileged position in society. Both factions agreed that such benefits could not be extended to the mulattoes, much less to the slaves. It was only in 1791 that the slaves rose en masse and began to fight for their rights.

Now that the black slaves were fighting for their own rights the revolution added a new racial dimension to the struggle. Until now blacks had been fighting blacks for the benefit of the white bourgeoisie and for the benefit of France. From 1791 until 1804 the blacks would fight only whites and in the interest of blacks (James 1963, 85-118).

Under the charismatic leadership and military genius of Toussaint L'Ouverture the black slaves succeeded in destroying the resistance of the plantation and slave owners in the north, overran the opposition of the free blacks and mulattoes in the south, and expelled successive invasions of French, English and Spanish troops sent to crush the revolution (Griffiths 1970). By the turn of the century Toussaint L'Ouverture was ready to start the work of social and economic reconstruction of a country literally devastated by ten years of revolution. The worst was still to come with the counterrevolutionary schemes of Napoleon Bonaparte (Ott 1973: 139-145).

In order to restore political and economic dominance over the island, Napoleon dispatched a most formidable military expedition headed by his own brother-in-law, General Leclerc. The purpose of the expedition was to crush the power of the revolutionary forces headed by black and mulatto generals, restore supremacy to the white bourgeoisie and re-establish slavery for the black masses. The bourgeois revolution in France had proclaimed its twin goals of freedom and equality for all. When the sans-culottes and the urban masses tried to extend such privileges to themselves, Bonaparte stepped in with the counter-revolution. Following the steps of the metropolis, the colonial and creole white bourgeoisie in Haiti had secured for themselves equality with the metropolitan bourgeoisie. The free blacks and mulattoes had tampered with those rights demanding equality with the creole bourgeoisie. When the black slaves proclaimed themselves free and demanded equality with the creole white and mulatto bourgeoisie, the revolution in the colony had gone too far and the counter-revolution in France made a supreme effort to halt its course (Logan 1968: 89).

Tousaint L'Ouverture, despite his charisma and his military genius, never understood that the racial and class struggle he was commanding could never succeed if the colonial links with France were maintained. Until his death in a French prison he continued to believe and trust that one day Napoleon would understand that the black slaves fought only for their freedom not against France. The interests of France, according to Napoleon and the white colonists, would best be served by re-establishing the supremacy of the white colonists and reducing the blacks to slavery. This, despite Napoleon's ambition, never happened (James 1963: 269-288).

Although the French troops, through guile and treachery, succeeded in sending Toussaint L'Ouverture into exile, they failed in subjugating the blacks and restoring slavery and dependence. Resistance to the white troops was general and unrelenting. The fighting on both sides became increasingly cruel and vicious. By 1803, Napoleon's troops, decimated by yellow fever, were forced to retreat from the island leaving behind more than 40,000 dead. Haiti was now totally in ruins. Indpendence was finally proclaimed in 1804. Haiti was the first black independent republic in the Americas. After independence, the black republic found itself isolated not only from France but from most other European countries and the United States. The Western world could come to terms with the French revolution, but it could not accept that black slaves could destroy white supremacy in Haiti and become the masters of their own destiny (Logan 1968: 94-103).

A cursory analysis of the historical events from 1790 to 1804 shows that the class structure and social organization of Haitian society were deeply affected. It seems reasonable to argue that the revolution was primarily anti-slavery, anti-plantation and anti-white more than it was anti-French. Nearly half a million black slaves worked in the plantations for some 30,000 whites who served the interests of France either as bureaucrats, government officials, soldiers or businessmen. The same whites that demanded equality and representation in the Estates General for the white bourgeoisie of Haiti, were totally oblivious to the fact that they were the masters and oppressors of half a million black slaves. When, in 1791, the slaves revolted en masse against the whites, their intention was to destroy an economic and political system that was oppressive and exploitative. They burned and looted the rich sugar, coffee and cotton plantations because these were the symbols of colonial exploitation. They pillaged the mansions of the whites and killed their wives and children because the whites were the instruments of oppression and the targets of their hate. They attacked and killed free blacks and mulattoes because these had come to identify themselves with the interests of the whites (Hall 1971: 136-151).

Slavery and plantations were the cornerstones of colonial Haiti. The mode of production and the social relations of the colonial society were conditioned by these two institutions. Moreover these same institutions specified the relations existing between the colonial and metropolitan societies. By destroying both institutions the blacks had unwittingly cut themselves loose from their condition of dependence on the metropolis. Toussaint L'Ouverture did not quite understand the scope and depth of the revolution when he tried to maintain Haiti's political association with France. Napoleon, however, did realize that domination over the colony could be maintained only by re-establishing the class system with its two main institutions, slavery and plantations. To this effect he sent some of his best troops to Haiti, with the purpose of eliminating Toussaint and subjugating the ex-slaves. His troops succeeded militarily in getting rid of Toussaint but failed politically to subdue the masses and return them to slavery (Ott 1973: 170-188).

With the elimination of the slavery and plantation systems, Haiti was ready to forge new social relations and new forms of productive activity that would provide the foundation for the new society. Unfortunately, the devastation of the means of production reached during the war, and the degree of disintegration of the colonial society were such that the reorganization of the new society became almost an impossible task unless outside help could be secured. Throughout the nineteenth century Haiti was relegated to a situation of abject isolation and neglect. A blockade of silence and prejudice was imposed around the nation that witnessed the first social revolution in the western hemisphere (James 1963: 391-418; Logan 1968: 94-103).

2. Class and Revolution in Cuba; 1952-1959

The events that took place in Cuba from 1952 to 1959 were on the surface quite different from those that produced the Haitian revolution in the eighteenth century. Cuba had gained political independence some fifty years before the revolution and there were no slaves to liberate. As in the Haitian revolution, however, the revolutionary process brought to Cuba new relations in production and a new reorganization of the class structure. To reach this objective the Cuban people in 1959, like the Haitians in 1804, had to undertake the costly and painful task of abrogating the relations of dependence that tied them, like an umbilical cord, to a metropolitan center. In the case of Cuba this meant cutting its nearly total dependence on the United States. This is what the Cuban revolution accomplished by the end of 1960 (Boorstein 1968; Sears 1964; Rodríguez 1983; Castro 1976).

The United States had been the dominant power in Cuba's political and economic life since the end of the Cuban-Hispanic war in 1898. Directly through military interventions, constitutional amendments and ambassadors-proconsuls, or indirectly through dictators, military threats and economic sanctions, the United States controlled the political system. Through investments, financing, trade, import-export quotas and agreements, U.S. control of the economy was almost total. In fifty years the United States had succeeded in implanting in Cuba a dependent capitalist system that would provide needed raw materials at lowest possible costs (Thomas 1971; Pérez 1978; Manitzas 1973; Leuchsering 1973: 25-69). Dependent capitalism created in Cuba a client-dominant class that identified itself with American interests more than with those of other Cubans (López 1973; O'Connor 1972; Bonachea and Valdés 1972).

The Cuban bourgeoisie was composed of two segments significantly different in terms of their wealth and power (Rodríguez 1983: 286-390; Merkx and Valdés 1972; Amaro and Lago 1971; Manitzas 1973b). The upper segment was composed of large land owners, bankers, financiers, industrial entrepreneurs, real estate developers and businessmen engaged mostly in the import-export trade. They were all white and mostly of Spanish descent, well-educated, had traveled extensively abroad particularly to the United States where they often had bank accounts and sometimes sent their children to school. They were Roman Catholics, politically conservative, moderately nationalist, and patronized the church, cultural institutions and politics at the national and local levels. The other segment of the bourgeoisie was composed of small owners, small businessmen, store owners, merchants and traders in the internal market, well-established professionals such as doctors, lawyers and engineers, government officials, bureaucrats and military officers. Most of them were also of Spanish descent, subscribed to Catholic practices, sent their children to private schools, competed for status with the other segment of the bourgeoisie and entered politics or the government as a means of rapidly accumulating wealth and gaining status. Both segments of the bourgeoisie shared a colonial subservient world view that Cuba's economy and polity could only develop if good relations were maintained with the United States. An educated guess would claim that around ten percent of the Cuban population could be classified in this category by 1959. There was also a burgeoning petit bourgeoisie composed of a variety of people engaged mostly in bureaucratic and white collar occupations, small independent merchants, shopkeepers, sales people, peasants with small land holdings, teachers and professionals, technicians with a trade or skill and a steady job. Perhaps the best distinguishing trait of this quasi-class was that its members had a secure source of income either through work, a small business, a profession or a skill. They sent their children to public schools, many of them were Catholics, they emulated the privileges and status of the upper bourgeoisie, supported populist political parties like the Auténtico and Ortodoxo parties and hoped for the implementation of social reforms, often promised to them before presidential elections. It would fair to estimate the number of people in this class at about fifteen percent of the population.

The rest of the population, nearly 75 percent of the total, could be classified as an "under-class." It comprised the bulk of the industrial urban and rural proletariat, the semi-skilled and unskilled laborers, the peasants in the countryside, the unemployed and underemployed in the cities and in the countryside and the unemployable, i.e., those without any trade or skills and illiterate. This latter group could only find work during the harvest season cutting sugar cane some three months a year for a minimum wage. This underclass was composed of a mixture of white Cubans of Spanish extraction and blacks and mulattoes (Sweezy and Huberman 1960; Zeitlin 1967; Thomas 1967; Wood 1969; O'Connor 1966). It was also a mixture of urban dwellers and peasants, of employed and unemployed, of literate and illiterate people. Their children attended public schools, many of them considered themselves Catholics, although they might not attend church ceremonies, and with the exception of participation in some labor organizations and in some political activities, their level of political participation was relatively low. Many Cubans were religiously and politically apathetic, having lost faith in the political and religious institutions of the society. Time after time politicians from the bourgeoisie had reneged on the promises they made before an election. Since the inception of the republic, all politicians, regardless of the manner by which they had obtained power, either through a coup or through popular vote, had engaged in the same corrupt practices and abuses (Yglesias 1980: 3-25).

Many Cubans of the underclass were aware that both dictators and presidents, despite their personal ambitions, were allowed to stay in power as long as they served the interests of the upper bourgeoisie and its allies. Whenever a dictator became a liability for the bourgeoisie and its allies, or a president became too independent or too weak to guarantee the required stability, the bourgeoisie and its allies would exert pressure to accelerate a transition to another style or would induce a change in personnel without altering the structure (Thomas 1971: 605-678).

The revolution of 1959 was seen by some as one more episode in the changes in personnel that had taken place in Cuban politics since 1933. Soon, however, Cubans began to realize that it was not a change in personnel or in cosmetic style that was taking place. The promises for reform made during the guerrilla campaign were being implemented. Moreover profound structural changes in the political and economic structures were contemplated. Such changes were immediately perceived as threatening the status and dominance of the upper bourgeoisie and its allies. The counter-revolution began to organize itself as early as July 1959. The upper and most of the middle bourgeoisie migrated to the United States with their wealth, children and skills. It recruited support from its allies at home and abroad to stop the revolutionary process. By the end of 1961 the counter-revolution had been almost totally defeated (Castro 1976: 51-62). The government of the United States was still convinced that it could choke the revolution by isolating Cuba politically and economically from the capitalist world. For over 30 years the American government has maintained an economic and political blockade of Cuba.

The revolution had started as a political rebellion against a dictatorial regime that was illegal and unconstitutional but protected the stability needed by dependent capitalism to function. While the revolution was fighting the military dictatorship of Batista it was widely supported by the middle bourgeoisie. When it threatened the system of dependent capitalism by implementing redistributive policies, the upper bourgeoisie and the U.S. proclaimed opposition to the objectives of the revolution and the middle class supported their position (Thomas 1967; Kula 1981). By then, however, the revolutionary process could count on the full-fledged support of the masses, and promptly embarked on a speedy dismantling of the system of dependent capitalism (Rodríguez 1965; Alroy 1973; Azicri and Moreno 1981).

Ever since independence from Spain, the Cuban economy had been tied to the United States. American companies owned the best productive lands, mining concerns, most of the sugar industry, the means of transportation and communication and most of the banking and insurance business. Furthermore, whatever portion of the economy was owned by Cuban nationals, it also depended on the U.S. markets and suppliers. The upper and middle bourgeoisie had adapted well to this client-condition and was generally well rewarded by this system of economic exploitation. When the revolution of 1959 posed a threat to American interests in Cuba, the bourgeoisie rallied behind them. Unlike the situation in Haiti, where the leaders of the revolution thought that they could dismantle the class system of plantation economy without antagonizing Napoleon and the French bourgeoisie, the leaders of the Cuban revolution understood as early as 1960 that restructuring the class system and altering relations of production could not be accomplished without interfering with American interests in Cuba. Unlike Toussaint L'Ouverture 150 years earlier, Fidel Castro understood that the system of domination of the upper bourgeoisie was intimately tied to the country's political and economic dependence on the United States, and that the class system could only be dismantled by cutting the ties that made Cuba's economy and political life dependent on the United States (Rodríguez 1961).

The reaction of the United States was confrontation and opposition to the revolution. It used all means available, short of direct military intervention, to stop the revolutionary process. Cuban exiles were recruited and trained by the CIA to launch in 1961 the ill-fated invasion of the Bay of Pigs (Szulc 1986: 532-561). Later that year Cuba sought and obtained economic and military support from the U.S.S.R. After the dramatic events of the missile crisis in October 1962 the United Stats tacitly agreed not to invade Cuba (Castro 1976: 56-57). However, it did not give up a policy of isolating Cuba from its neighbors and from Western Europe. Such a policy was reminiscent of the way Haiti was isolated by France after the revolution of 1804. Early in 1961 the U.S. had severed diplomatic relations with Cuba and in 1964 persuaded Latin American countries to cut economic and diplomatic ties and to impose an economic embargo on Cuba. Although the embargo was finally called off in 1975 by most Latin countries, the United States still enforces it today.

Unlike Haiti, the fate of the Cuban revolution was not arrested because of the policies of isolation imposed from the outside. Thirty years after the seizure of power, the revolution can claim to have fully institutionalized a different political and economic system and to have laid the foundations for the creation of a new social order based on cultural values that are quite different from those held under dependent capitalism (Halebski and Kirk 1985). To be sure, Cuva is still an underdeveloped country and far from being self-sufficient. However, no part of Cuba, with the exception of Guantanamo Bay, is owned or controlled by foreign interests. The Cuban people own the means of production for the country and its natural resources. Social and economic rewards are distributed in a fairly egalitarian way for the benefit of the collectivity. The Cuban people, despite serious scarcities in the availability of some consumer goods, are today better fed, healthier, better educated, and have more job security than they ever had (Benjamin et al. 1984).

3. Class and Revolution in the Dominican Republic; 1961-1965

Although in this paper only the revolutions of 1959 in Cuba and that of Haiti in 1804 are considered full-fledged revolutions, there were other uprisings (Puerto Rico 1868, Dominican Republic 1865, Cuba 1868) and rebellions (Cuba 1895, 1933; and Dominican Republic 1965) that shared some of the same characteristics as a true revolution. However, all these revolutionary efforts were thwarted by internal exhaustion or crushed by superior military forces from outside. Of all these cases I would like to discuss briefly the Dominican Revolution of 1965.

Like most other countries in the Caribbean the Dominican Republic became increasingly dependent on the United States in the Twentieth Century (Brea 1983; Boin and Serrulle 1981). United States forces occupied the country from 1916 to 1924 and after they departed, the country was left with the Trujillo dictatorship for over 30 years (Lozano 1976; Knight 1939; Cassá 1984). After the death of Trujillo, the Dominican people succeeded in electing a constitutional regime which was ousted in 1963 after only eight months in power. The country was thrown back again to civilian-military juntas. During this period, as during the thirty years Trujillo was dictator, the United States maintained friendly relations with the country and indirectly played a dominant role in the political and economic life of the nation.

The class composition of the Dominican Republic during the dictatorship of Trujillo and in its immediate aftermath resembled the class composition of Cuba under the first dictatorship of Batista. The small upper bourgeoisie that existed before Trujillo came to power continued to co-exist with the dictator. Trujillo did not allow it to expand nor did he allow too much encroachment of American interests in the country. Trujillo did allow the emergence of a middle bourgeoisie composed of members of his own family, government bureaucrats, professionals, military officers and a few businessmen and entrepreneurs. The distinguishing trait of this group was their loyalty to Trujillo. The size of the upper and middle bourgeoisie could be estimated at about ten percent of the population. The rest of the population made an underclass of urban dwellers and peasants most of them illiterate and unemployed who had adapted to a life of oppression and scarcity (Bosch 1983a; Bosch 1983b).

Until his death in 1961 Trujillo ruled the country with an iron fist. He owned most of the economy and dominated the political life of the country for thirty years. Almost until his death he was a good friend and ally of the United States. After his death, the middle bourgeoisie created by him attempted to stay in power using different political strategies. The government of the United States was sympathetic to the idea of keeping this group in power since it would implement policies similar to those of Trujillo and would maintain stability. If this group was not able to gain power through the electoral process, a military coup would be in order. And so, after only eight months in office the government freely elected by the people in the first free election in the country was deposed by a military coup. Despite protestations to the contrary, the American government recognized the new unconstitutional regime only a few weeks after the coup (Martin 1966; Bosch 1964).

The uprising of 1965 began as a civilian-military revolt to restore the short-lived experiment in constitutional democracy of 1963. Again, what was started by an elite group as an uprising demanding certain political rights and the restoration of constitutional government, soon turned into a mass popular rebellion demanding drastic structural changes in the economy and in the social organization (Moreno 1970; Gleijeses 1978).

The Dominican bourgeoisie soon realized that the fighting that was taking place in the streets of Santo Domingo did not represent merely two factions of the military fighting against each other. It was rather a struggle for power between two classes and their forces. On the one side there were the forces defending the privileges of the bourgeoisie with their generals and military hardware. On the other side stood the masses of Santo Domingo with only a few weapons, but in great numbers, demanding their rights. The battle for Santo Domingo was bloody, uneven and fierce. When the bourgeoisie realized that the masses posed a real threat to their existence, it appealed for help from the American embassy (Moreno 1982).

After three days of fighting in the streets of Santo Domingo, the rebel forces with overwhelming popular support were ready to launch the last attack against the stronghold of the loyalist forces at the San Isidro air base. At this point, 23,000 American troops landed in Santo Domingo to contain the revolutionary upsurge. Various excuses provided by American officials, at different times, to justify the armed intervention in a small helpless country were soon discredited by American journalists working in Santo Domingo (Szulc 1965; Draper 1968). A more convincing explanation suggests that the American government could accept various changes in personnel in Dominican affairs, such as dictators, juntas and even some forms of liberal democracy, but could not tolerate a revolution. A revolution would bring about new relations in production and new class alignments that would destroy the relations of dependency on the United States. A revolution with mass popular support represented a threat to American interests in the country since such a process by necessity would attempt to improve the conditions of the people and preserve the integrity of the nation and its national resources (Cassá 1984: 161-185; Franco 1966).

4. Conclusion

In summary, if a revolution is a drastic process of change that profoundly alters the social structure of a society by reconstituting its relations in production, and by redefining its social relations, then in the context of dependent societies, like those of the Caribbean, a revolution can only take place by dismantling the condition of dependence that created and maintained such relations. In other words, revolutions in the Caribbean must be conceptualized as taking place at two levels at the same time. The first level will include a struggle to subvert the domination of the client-dominant class, represented by dictators, military juntas or even civilian regimes. The second level includes a challenge to a metropolitan hegemonic power that maintains close economic and political dominance over the relations in production. The struggle at these two levels must be simultaneous since they support each other, and a challenge to one will be perceived as a threat by the other. Both France in 1804 and the United States in 1959 realized that the challenge of Toussaint L'Overture and of Fidel Castro to the local client-dominant classes was a threat to their hegemonic dominance over their respective colonies. By the same token, it was only when the leaders of the two revolutions directed the fight against the forces representing the metropolitan power that they finally succeeded in defeating the local power structure. Aborted revolutions are those in which the revolutionary forces succeed in defeating their enemies in one level but not in the other. The Dominican uprising of 1965 provides us with an excellent example. The rebel forces had already defeated the forces of the bourgeoisie. The American military intervention took place to salvage the bourgeoisie from total destruction. In cases of successful revolutions, when the counter-revolution has been defeated it is possible that the hegemonic metropolis will attempt to defeat the revolution by policies of isolation. The cases of Haiti and Cuba are good illustrations.

Disjunctive Justice and Revolutionary Movements: The 4.19 (Sa-il-gu) Upheaval and the Fall of the Syngman Rhee Regime in South Korea*

QUEE-YOUNG KIM**

ABSTRACT

The state-centered structural approach to the study of social revolutions neglects to consider moral factors and the processes of revolutionary movements. This chapter examines the stages by which protest movements develop into a revolution. I argue that social movements can best be understood in terms of three nonstructural concepts: disjunctive justice, power deflation and illegitimate coercion. The conceptual model is developed from an empirical study of the Sa-il-gu upheaval in the spring of 1960 that ousted the Syngman Rhee regime in South Korea.

UNDER WHAT CONDITIONS, and in what way, do rebellions, revolts and protest movements lead to a revolution? How shall we explain the process by which political leadership, policies and institutions are radically transformed by violent means? Existing studies provide little guidance to help us answer these questions. In fact, as a recent review of the literature on collective behavior and social movements has pointed out, the dynamics of collective action are the least understood field in the social sciences. (McAdam, McCarthy and Zald, 1988; also see Goldstone, 1980). In the field of collective behavior in general and revolutionary movements in particular, there are several problems that retard progress in this direction. This paper uses a case study of Korea to discuss some of these problems and highlight the importance of the moral factor in the revolutionary process.

Revolutionary Movements

"A Revolution," according to Huntington, "is a rapid, fundamental, and violent domestic change in the dominant values and myths of a society, in its

---

* I have benefited from helpful comments and editorial advice from Professors Garth Massey of the Department of Sociology and two anonymous reviewers. I would like to thank the Department of Sociology, University of Wyoming for institutional support during the period in which I wrote this chapter.

** Department of Sociology, University of Wyoming, Laramie, Wyoming 82071, U.S.A.

political institutions, social structure, leadership, and government activity and politices'' (1968: 264). Defining revolution in this way as a phenomenon, a kind of historical moment, makes it difficult for anyone to analyze the process of revolutionary transformation from one stage to the next. In the multivariate language there are no variations in the dependent variable over time. One needs, however, to identify the different levels of a revolutionary situation in terms of whether the conflict between social forces and the state is legally bound (e.g. whether existing institutional authority such as government or court decisions would be sufficient to resolve the major disputes or not) or constitutional (e.g. whether the existing institutional authority is unable to resolve the questions of who should rule, how and why); and whether violence is used in constitutional conflict to settle the issue.

A revolutionary movement is a series of social movements that defies the political authority in public and aims to change the policies, leadership and state organization by extralegal and violent means. It is different from a *coup d'etat* in the degree of openness, the source of mobilization and the extent of participation in the revolutionary struggle. A revolutionary movement might or might not include military participation, but coups can happen without any social movement. A revolutionary movement may lead to revolution if the revolutionary organization and leadership seize the state and transform social structure and values in a violent and fundamental way. A revolutionary movement may or may not follow important fundamental changes in culture and social structure, although commonly they do.

There are successful as well as unsuccessful revolutionary movements. In May 1968, French students and workers staged violent demonstrations and strikes to change the policies of the De Gaulle government, but without much success (see e.g., Aron 1969; Lefebvre 1969). In the late 1960s, American students, blacks, intellectuals and many others opposed American involvement in the Vietnam war, as well as racial discrimination and other social injustices. Changes in policies and, to some extent, leadership was brought about, but little change was made in the basic principles of political institutions. (see, e.g., Lipset 1972; Wood 1974). In the early 1960s, many Koreans lodged protests against electoral fraud, leading to changes in political leadership, policies, and to an important extent, political institutions, including the collapse of the ruling party, the reelection of the entire National Assembly, and substantial change in the distribution of power between the National Assembly and the Executive Branch. But there was no change in the principles of political institutions, nor in social structure or values (Kim, 1983). In 1989, many Chinese students demanded democracy, staging demonstrations, without them developing into a revolutionary outcome.

In its basic form, a revolutionary movement shares the same characteristics as collective behavior and social movements. It is spontaneous, public, group behavior, surprising to many. The goals of the movement evolve to change either the policies or the leadership of the government, and, if possible, the political institutions as well. When rebellions, riots, revolts, demonstrations, protest movements and mass movements develop in response to a common concern, with or without any ideological unity or organizational command but in unified opposition to the political authority, then the phenomena could be called a revolutionary movement. A revolutionary movement, like an individual, defines its character in the choice it makes. Therefore, one has to locate the turning points, define the alternatives which confronted the movement, and try to understand the contexts in which important changes occur.

A revolutionary movement is not the work of a single individual or a single social group. Nor does it occur in one apocalyptic convulsion. Different groups participate in the process at different points in time, and different groups in the government suppress and react to these challenges in different ways. Therefore analysis of revolutionary movements must contrast state and society in a dialectical relationship. A revolutionary movement is a series of activities by a group of actors to change political practices, policies, and the leadership of the government by violent means. It is a social movement with a specific political goal of changing the authority by defying it, intentional or otherwise, in the form of demonstrations, protests, riots and rebellion.

Many theories of revolution emphasize structural over cultural and moral factors. Skocpol (1979) and Tilly (1978) provide important examples. Skocpol's study of revolutions stressed the importance of the state and emphasized the structural determinants of outcomes. Despite its significant contributions to the understanding of historical cases, it does not analyze the crucial question of the dynamics of interaction between the state and social forces during the revolutionary process. The analytic scheme that served well for these historical revolutions may not do well for the contemporary movements, especially in developing societies.

Tilly (1978) defines the revolutionary situation in terms of multiple sovereignty and "catnet"—the extent to which people of similar social categories can act together and mobilize the necessary resources. In the great French, Russian and Chinese revolutions where "counter-government" or "government in exile" overthrew an incumbent regime, multiple sovereignty clearly was present and created a revolutionary situation. But revolutions, the violent and sudden overthrow of a government, do occur without an institutionalized form of multiple sovereignty or extant civil war. In order to explain why and how protest movements develop into a revolution one has to step back and ask why and how "multiple sovereignty" conditions emerge in the first place, why and how different social groups act together under certain conditions, and why under a variety of conditions the same groups fight against each other. The assumption that people of common social categories will become revolutionary depending upon the availability of resources is not tenable. The ability of groups of individuals to act together must be questioned as the basis for the analysis of revolutionary situations rather than accepted as given. Resource mobilization may be less crucial than Tilly assumes it to be.

The purpose of this article is to offer an alternative conceptual scheme to the structural approach. Building upon the arguments of Liu (1988) that the relative ability to mobilize resources was less crucial than the legitimacy of the use of violence during the constitutional conflict in determining the revolutionary processes and outcomes in Iran and Poland, it presents a conceptual framework for the analysis of the revolutionary process and applies it to the case of the Korean student-citizen protest movements that overthrew the Syngman Rhee regime in 1960. In particular, it argues that this social movement can best be understood in terms of three nonstructural concepts: disjunctive justice, power deflation and illegitimate coercion.

The 4.19 (Sa-il-gu) Revolt in Brief

Since the independence of Korea from Japanese colonialism in 1945, the territorial division of Korea along the 38th parallel in 1948, through the Korean War (1950-1953) and subsequent years of a devastated economy (1953-1960), Syngman Rhee dominated political leadership in South Korea. He repeatedly used dictatorial methods under a democratic constitution to hold onto power. In 1954 he and the ruling Liberal Party (*Chayudang*) imposed on the National Assembly a constitutional amendment that would allow him to remain President for life. Despite Rhee's efforts at total political domination, the political opposition gathered enough votes in 1956 to elect a Vice-President of their choice. In the 1958 general elections the opposition Democratic Party (*Minjudang*) obtained almost a two-thirds majority in the National Assembly. The Liberal Party attempted to turn the electoral tide by draconian measures. In the name of National Security, key opposition figures were arrested, others harrassed. In 1960, the Rhee administration and its party rigged the Presidential election using terrorist tactics and oppressive measures. A relatively free press championed the cause for "democracy and freedom" and the public became outraged. A series of students' demonstrations in several cities escalated the political crisis into civil violence. On April 19 (*Sa-il-gu*) 1960, students from nearly all of Seoul's colleges and universities and from many high schools staged spectacular and massive demonstrations. Several policemen and hundreds of youth were killed. Unable to control the violent upheaval the government declared martial law and relied on the Korean Army to keep order in the streets. University professors, defying a military ban on public activity, took to the streets demanding the resignation of President Rhee. Enthusiastic crowds from various walks of life, especially the young, occupied the streets throughout the night of April 25, 1960. More and massive demonstrations were rumored to be in the offing. To prevent what one official called, "a massacre, a sea of fire and blooshed," the military "remained neutral" (Kim Chong-yol, 1973) in what they considered an unfair power struggle engineered by a few ambitious politicians and did not open fire upon the demonstrators. The American Army Command in Korea that had operational authority over the Korean Army would not authorize a major crackdown. President Rhee hurriedly announced his resignation the following morning over the radio. Thus came the end of his regime.

The event is called the Sa-il-gu (April 19th) Uprising or the April Revolution. A Korean historian wrote:

> The April Revolution was the first in the history of Korea wherein a people armed with nothing but their bare fists succeeded in overthrowing an oppressive government. The leading role in this revolution was performed by students. Their loss of faith in the established generation and its political order led them to take their position in the vanguard of the April 1960 revolutionary struggle. At the same time, the revolution could not have been won without the wholehearted support of the people. (Lee, 1984: 385)

Disjunctive Justice

The relationship between the state and society is normative. "The polity," Daniel Bell writes, "is the arena of social justice and power: the control of the legitimate use of force and the regulation of conflict in order to achieve the particular conceptions of justice embodied in a society's traditions or in its constitution, written or unwritten" (1976: 11). The state forces its ends upon society and justifies its means but a regime cannot endure, "for even a week through force alone. It needs the cement of morality." (Trotsky 1942: 81) "Morality serves interests; and often social and political interests are contradictory." (Trotsky 1942: 21).

In general, men act not in response to situations but in response to their ideas of situations which are colored by the moral order of the society, a faith in the principles of right and wrong and the understanding that practices should generally conform to expectations. These ideas determine the form of the assault which otherwise could take many different forms. People act, not so much from material interests, but out of their own concept of justice (Camus 1956). The way rebels justify their own behavior is more important in understanding rebellion than inferring an unconscious, hidden meaning to their action resulting from a change in relation to economic conditions. In short, revolt is an outcome of critical, moral consciousness, a creative action to better the human condition. The relevant context in which to study revolt is not relative deprivation, but disjunctive justice; not suffering, but the moral order of society; not economics, but political culture.

The contradiction between social and political interests has been termed disjunctive justice. It appears in the form of "mutual recrimination among leaders in society, who accuse each other of violating the rules of fair play and use this as a justification for not following such rules themselves." (Stinchcombe 1965: 175).

The concept of justice ranks high in society's hierarchy of values. However, justice is ambiguous in meaning and discrepant from one social group to another. Only those who are able to articulate the notion of discrepancy between principle and practice and define it as a contradiction in light of some general moral principle, can indeed create a revolt. What transforms the status quo into intolerable and unjust conditions is a new definition of the situation through typification. What compels one to act in a political society is a moral outrage over practices that contradict a principle, a feeling that something is not right in light of some image or model. One commonly held notion of justice is the idea of utilitarian justice, based on what Weber calls "instrumental rationality," a notion that the expedient means justifies the public ends, largely upheld by those in authority. Another image of justice is usually upheld at a particular time by those who feel oppressed and suppressed and arises from contrasting the practices of utilitarian justice with the principle. Thus, the fundamental spirit that guides the dissent is "substantive rationality." This conflict between two divergent notions of justice is what is here called "disjunctive justice."

Disjunctive justice is a concept denoting a contradiction between principle and practice; it hinges on a sense of righteousness, a faith that one's judgment is right in comparing the principle of political ligitimacy with the practices of leadership and policies. It assumes the existence of a normative structure for making policy decisions compatible with the expectations inferred from implicit or explicit principles. Justice prevails if the obligations between authorities and subjects are reciprocated. The more the authorities act in conformity with generalized expectations, the more powerful is their legitimacy. The expectations are, in turn, shaped by cultural traditions and structural changes of the society. A revolt is a way of reminding the authorities of the principles and of dramatizing claims made upon the authorities. In this sense, revolt is not a threat to social order so much as to political leadership. It is a dramatic occasion for the redefinition of a society's moral order.

The probability that disjunctive justice will lead to conflict is conditional to the individual's acceptance or rejection of the prevailing principles and practices. As schematically presented in Table 1, several logical possibilities emerge from this kind of moral choice.

Table 1
Disjunction between Moral Principle and Political Practice

Response	Moral Principle	Political Practice
Conform	Accept	Accept
Reform	Reject	Accept
Rebellion	Accept	Reject
Revolution	Reject	Reject

If one accepts the moral principle that governs the instrumental or substantive rationality, and also the political practices that emanate from the principle, then one is very likely to conform to political authority. Reform movements are similar to rebellion, but they are different from revolution in that reformers basically accept the political practice—not that it is good but that it is to be changed as a logical result of changing moral principle. Rebellion, in fact, attempts to reaffirm the moral principle that guides political practices. Revolution attempts to reconstitute a new moral principle and create a new order.

For disjunctive justice to affect the occurrence of protest, it must fit within existing contradiction and polarization of moral principle; that is, the beliefs that will contribute to collective protest are those that help explain and translate the injustice and immorality of politics to an angry population, and must be given concrete substance by precipitating factors, when political authorities contradict moral principle with political practice. When the authorities fail to provide security for the people, despite declared promises, and when they use their offices to advance their own wealth and power, then strong moral anguish will arise against the regime. If the constitution guarantees both representation and participation in politics, and yet the means to these ends are thwarted forcefully and arbitrarily, then revolt is likely to occur.

In a cultural tradition that stresses moral orthodoxy, political antinomy and contradictions between principle and practice appear exaggerated. Since, ultimately, it is religion or ideology that provides moral energy, in countries where the religious or ideological traditions are strong revolt and rebellion stemming from moral outrage seem common. Political alienation of intellectuals from particularly centralized states turns debates on disjunctive justice (e.g. corruption of government officials, rigging of elections) into counter-justice; instead of trying to tinker with some of the parts of political society, a passion to overthrow the regime will prevail.

The substance of the moral issue can indicate the character of the movement: socialist or democratic. If socio-economic inequality is the issue, then socialist movement will develop. If political liberty is considered unjustly denied, then a democratic movement will evolve. In either case, when moral issues are simplified, a claim to justice is established. Then, in the union of simplication of moral issues and claims to justice, a commitment to action spreads, and a revolt is born. If the underlying sense of moral order is quite strong, different social groups can more easily come together for a common cause.

During the process of a social movement, different social groups can come to the realization of disjunctive justice at different points in time. The conception of what is right and wrong, decent and indecent, humane and inhumane may change through the interaction between social force and power structure. The original conception of justice can be exaggerated and undermined, depending on the nature of the conflict. Revolutionary movements, in this sense, are radically different from internal war, where resources and mobilization decide the final outcome, rather than moral consciousness. No political regime ever exhausts all of its resources to counter a revolt. (Consider for example the 1979 Iranian revolution. See among others, Arjomand, 1988.) It falls by its own moral weight. A simplistic corollary would be that the amount of violence necessary to change a political regime is relative to the moral calibre of the political leadership.

The legal organization of the Rhee regime was a system of democratic sovereignty with a constitutional division of power among the executive, judiciary and legislative branches. The legitimacy of the regime was based on national plebiscite. This view became the official doctrine of political socialization across the entire school system and an accepted premise of institutional authority.

In reality, however, political power was concentrated in the hands of President Rhee. His administration ruled people with legalistic judgment disregarding the autonomy of legislative authority. His claim to the right to rule came not as a people's choice but from his credential as the leader of the independence movement prior to 1945. By 1960, Rhee was 85 and his regime had become lethargic; corruption was rampant. Journalists, writers and professors criticized the political leaders for their moral failings, perhaps to fill a void in public purpose and largely as a duty to set things right according to moral principles and the ideals of democracy. Democracy was the catchword, a kind of counter-justice that inspired students. The idea that everyone, especially the students themselves whose family backgrounds were of mostly common origins, could become somebody and participate in decision-making under principles of equal opportunity excited them. Democracy was a broad Utopian and vague concept as used by students in 1960. Students demonstrated in large numbers, acting out of acute consciousness that the government used repressive measures, including a rigged election, to maintain itself in power and generally failed to live up to the doctrine of democracy. (Democracy in its Korean translation, *minjujui*, means people making decisions.) Socialized into the ethos of nationalism in a newly-independent nation, students embodied symbolically the national consciousness. Their demands for a new election received overwhelming moral support from the press both at home and abroad. Several days of continuing demonstrations kept up the climactic mood on the marchers and maintained youthful enthusiasm. People in mostly urban areas supported the cause in a number of different ways, escalating the crisis. A violent confrontation between protesters and police on April 19, 1960 made it logistically impossible for the regime to "manage" the crisis within the legal constitutional framework. Martial law was declared and henceforth the survival of the regime hung on the use of force.

Power Deflation

One of the useful ideas for explaining a revolutionary situation is Parsons' (1967a) comparison of the process by which banks create money to the process by which power is generated in a polity. He compared loyal support and voting for a political group to depositing money in a bank. Political leaders create power on the basis of an original deposit of loyalty for a certain period of time during which most people will not suddenly demand their money back. No politicians can meet all their obligations instantaneously. Creating legitimate power is like expanding credit and loans on the basis of mutual trust and confidence. Creating money is inflationary if it changes the purchasing power of money. If the goods and services on the market expand simultaneously with the increase in money, there will be no inflation. Deflation occurs when too great a volume of goods and services chases too little money. Money loses its purchasing power and political power no longer rests on trust and confidence. Power deflation is the condition where the social order depends increasingly upon the maintenance and deployment of force by the authorities.

Parsons (1967a; 1967b) and Johnson (1966; 1982) suggest that revolution is like power deflation, a withdrawal of trust and confidence, a "run on the bank", characterized by too much political participation in weakened political institutions, a kind of democratic distemper and a revolution of rising expectations unleashed by disintegration of common values. This view leads to the mistaken conclusion that revolutions are the outcome of cultural disintegration. (Tilly 1978 and Skocpol 1979). To be sure, the effectiveness of political power depends on the trust and confidence of voters. But bankers can and do lose money due to misjudgment and greed and thus invite a run on the bank. Abuse of trust and confidence leads to political bankruptcy. Just as the availability of goods and services on the market determine the purchasing power of money, the effectiveness of political power is dependent upon the trust and confidence of voters in the political system. It is not the overwhelming demands and expectations that the government cannot meet that creates a revolutionary situation but a failure of leadership and the weakness of the state.

In a way one can argue that revolts are produced not necessarily by the rebels but by the authorities. The fundamental cause of revolt, then, is more to be found in the exercise of authority than anywhere else.

From 1953 to 1960, historical, international and institutional forces in South Korea created two contradictory tendencies: while the regime was drastically weakened by the destruction of the Korean War, it was moving more and more toward dictatorial rule; students, intellectuals and professionals developed a kind of institutional university-press nexus through which they launched their assault on the regime.

The Korean War (1950-53) destroyed nearly twice the value of the 1953 level GNP (Bank of Korea, 1955), the economy was depressed and unemployment rates in cities ran as high as thirty percent in some cases. The government, despite of its overall responsibility for the national welfare, did not do anything: there were no plans or visions for economic development. Foreign aid from the United States kept the economy afloat. But in 1958, the U.S. cut the funds by half, from $400 to $200 million a year, barely enough to keep a few essential bureaus operating.

The Rhee regime found itself strapped for cash in its electoral competition with the popular oppositions. It forced "contributions" from reluctant merchants. A high rate of inflation fueled the discontent of salaried and service workers. In fact the regime alienated the entire urban sector and relied increasingly on rural support. But the farmers, mostly in smallholding family units, were no major political force. Their status was local and interests were parochial. The manufacturing and retail trade were not yet the big business of the society. Universities, newspapers and political parties were national in their influence.

After the 1958 election which the opposition practically won, the regime resorted to force to maintain itself in power. Police became tools of political campaigns and outright suppression. The more force was used to command compliance, the greater the resistance to it became widespread.

After April 19, 1960 when the military took over the task of maintaining order in the streets, the conflict within the ruling structure escalated and polarized into a power struggle between those who would argue for "strong" measures as opposed to those who were conciliatory and appeared "weak". The results were almost a paralysis in the decision-making process and a naked exposure of the president as the ultimate agent for authority and responsibility. It seemed as if he stood alone against a sea of opposition.

Illegitimate Coercion

Why and under what conditions did the violence committed by the government upon its people become illegitimate and ineffective while the violence committed collectively by people against the government became legitimate and morally right?

It is well recognized that the state is "an organization that controls the principal means of coercion within a given territory" (Tilly 1975: 638). "The possession of a true monopoly over the legitimate use of force allows the authorities to exercise control through coercion, of which the use of force is the final and extreme form in a hierarchy of means" (Johnson 1982: 31). The last phase of revolutionary movements is usually marked by a condition in which the state resorts to physical force, the "most intrinsically effective of all means of coercion" (Parsons 1967a: 238), but fails to make it work.

The use of force must be legitimate and effective. Legitimacy refers to the degree to which the exercise of political authority by individuals through a set of institutions is regarded as right and appropriate. Effectiveness can be gauged by the strength of the power structure, its achievement of public goals, efficient use or threat of force. Organizational efficiency, the degree of cohesiveness among the political elites, bureaucratic capability and military strength are all measures of effectiveness that have important implications for the government's capacity to maintain political order. Of these qualities, the perception that force will be "backed up" by force and public opinion seem most important.

The political authority has the power to use violence in order to maintain social order. But the crucial point is not the capability to use violence, nor the magnitude, but the justification of it. Once it loses this justification by employing its force "unfairly," then the rebels can justify their fight against the "illegal regime."

An irony of political life is that force rarely appears justified, especially when used by those who have a complete monopoly of it. The magnitude of violence is limited and conditioned by the moral contours of political leadership rather than the available means of force. Perhaps the surest way to hasten the demise of a regime is to provoke it to use violence in a context that appears unwarranted and intentional, rather than accidental and inevitable. According to Chalmers Johnson, only "when force is used by authorities in a manner understood or expected by those sharing the system of values, i.e., in a way to which all value-sharers are committed, is it said to be legitimate" (1982: 30).

To be sure, legitimacy is a function of value structure. But it seems a folly to believe that there is a system of values to which all value-sharers are committed. In general, legitimacy is the function of moral evaluation of the exercise of power and in particular the use of force. It is not the national value consensus that makes the coercion illegitimate but a "moral majority" a dominant public opinion created by an elite of press corps, intellectuals, and an international press opinion as well as the perception and judgment of how, for instance, killing protesters is justified, that determines the moral sanction of the use of force.

The use of force becomes ineffective when it is used after power deflation, where trust and confidence in the authorities have evaporated to the extent that the exercise of power is futile and institutionally the authority of the body politic is not truly intact, that is, the civilian authorities are deadlocked at the level where decisions are to be enforced and where the armed forces cannot be trusted to obey civil authorities.

If the political leaders can use the army and police successfully to coerce people to their will, the state will continue to persist but in a new level, producing a "police state" (e.g., South Africa). Political oppositions can develop into underground forces or guerillas, thus creating a condition of "multiple sovereignty."

By April 20, the *Sa-il-gu* uprising had gained moral superiority over state repression, and thus made the use of coercion illegimate. On the issue of killing more than a hundred demonstrators, the government was on the defensive and the oppositions believed the decision unjustifiable. As more people condemned the action of the police, the more righteous the uprising appeared. The quantitative public support, which by now spread to heterogenous urban citizens of almost all walks of life, transformed the quality of the protest movement. The stunning demonstrations organized by university professors in Seoul and the massive crowds that accompanied them compelled the government to use force, but this time force could not be used.

The Korean government could not enlist the military in any major way to control the demonstrators without American approval. In fact, during the Korean war, the Rhee government transferred military operational command authority to the United Nations Command primarily under the influence of the United States Military Command in Korea. The United States Government under the Eisenhower administration condemned the Rhee regime for its failure to practice democracy and urged Rhee to, "take necessary and effective action aimed at protecting democratic rights of freedom of speech, of assembly, of the press as well as preserving the secrecy of the ballot and preventing unfair discrimination against political opponents of the party in power'' (New York Times, April 20, 1960). The Rhee regime collapsed because it could not use the army for its own defense against the mounting opposition from home and abroad.

Discussion and Conclusion

The *Sa-il-gu* upheaval was a unique event in modern Korean history. It was the first mass movement that overthrew a regime and no subsequent similar protests have been successful in repeating the same outcome. The event is a special case of revolutionary movement. The overall pattern of collective action is amenable to sociological analysis and empirical generalizations.

The revolutionary movement of *Sa-il-gu* developed from a situation of disjunctive justice, a condition that arose from the ideological mobilization of the university-press nexus against contradictory policies of the state. The fraudulent election galvanized the collective consciousness of the educated class in urban areas. The authorities could not control illegal but massive student demonstrations due to the weakness of the bureaucratic-police administration and the necessary resources available to the government. Power deflation prevailed especially after the violent confrontation between the protesters and police. Martial law was declared. The civilian authorities relied upon the military to maintain political order over the opposition that developed into a kind of moral majority whose opinions and actions already received public support from the greater part of the urban areas and from the international community, especially from the United States. Any further use of force was considered illegitimate, unthinkable and ineffective. The martial law command maintained a strict neutrality, which meant the withdrawal of the army's support for the regime. Finding no alternative, Rhee gave up his fight and his regime fell. The main lesson is that no protest will ever grow into a revolution unless and until the scenarios of disjunctive justice are followed by power deflation and illegitimate coercion.

In general, the following propositions can be used to explain the conditions and processes that transform a revolt into a revolutionary movement:

1. A revolutionary movement originates in the form of demonstrations protest movements, riots, marches, rebellions or revolts that occur within concrete historical contexts and are conditioned in their development by the relationship between the social and the political structure.

2. A revolutionary movement occurs under conditions of contradiction between an authority system and a cultural system, appearing in the form of a sense of injustice expressed through public opinion, and in conjunction with the declining legitimacy of the authority.

3. The goals and duration of a revolutionary movement depend upon ideological and material supports in the larger society, including national and international opinion.

4. Outcomes of a revolutionary movement are dependent upon authority responses and the transactions between social force and political authority. The most critical juncture is the use of violence, especially its timing, legitimacy and effectiveness.

5. The development of a revolutionary movement can be measured by the ratio between the extent of dissociation among important members of the power structure, fission between, for instance, the civilian leadership and the military commanders, and the degree of association among the institutional leaders of society, each undermining the legitimacy of the authority while promoting the cause of the movement.

6. If the established authorities are divided among themselves and unable to suppress discontent without using violence, and if the use of violence becomes illegitimate and ineffective, the revolutionary movement becomes successful.

The idea of disjunctive justice and the primacy of authority as the source of revolutionary impulse rather than class structure *per se* helps us to predict that those who watch the moral basis of authority, such as students, intelligentsia, intellectuals, or religious figures will be the first candidates for revolution and convinces us that people do things for the sake of public righteousness as much as for their own benefit.

Disjunctive justice is a dialectical synthesis of moral consciousness and ideological contradiction. Therefore, it is more likely to appear as a revolutionary condition in societies such as the Confucian, Shiite Islamic or Puritan where cultural tradition is steeped in moralistic orthodoxy. The outcome of revolution wrought by disjunctive justice would be some attempts, like the Glorious Revolution, to set things right that had gone wrong, (continuation of parliamentary government and the rule of law in England) and would not herald the kind of historical progress that Marx envisioned. In fact, the outcome can be quite conservative rather than progressive. Centralized and weak states are more likely to prompt revolt than decentralized and strong states. If the government has assumed the overall power over a wide range of national and individual matters, so will follow for better or worse the sense of responsibility. The more visible the power is, the more blame for misfortunes will quickly escalate to the center of power. The Rhee regime was repressive and had a precarious grasp on power. This kind of regime will be more vulnerable to the kind of moral outrage than many other authoritarian regimes.

What does the focus on process rather than structure contribute to the understanding of the origins and outcomes of revolutionary movements? How does the focus on society-state relationship lead ot the future study of revolutionary movements? Many attempts to discover the structural origins of revolution failed due to a mistaken notion that there is a threshold, a kind of "political boiling point," that one can identify and quantify. (see Almond 1973:35).

Neither change nor stability, in themselves, offer an explanation for the conditions of revolutionary movements. Structural factors do not operate directly upon social behavior but are mediated through the process of social interaction. The dynamic process of revolt is the result of interaction, bounded and channelled by various structural factors which give rise to emergent qualities and events. Structural changes set the stage and provide opportunities, but only specific interactive processes determine the outcome of a revolutionary movement. In attempting to account for concrete conflict situations, attention needs to be paid both to structural and processual factors.

The social origins of a revolutionary movement cannot be understood without analysis of the structural positions of the various groups, yet political struggles central to the revolutionary movement itself cannot be explained strictly in structural terms. Likewise, the causes and consequences of the revolutionary movement cannot be comprehended without a knowledge of social structure and its dynamics; economic conditions, intellectual alienation, and political decisions, which tend to be at variance with the expectations that logically arise from a structural perspective. Explaining the immediate circumstances of a revolutionary situation means analyzing the immediate issues, the extent of dissociation among the members of the power structure, the degree of association among social forces, the exchange of actions and reactions, the changing capability of the authority to command compliance from the people and the changing legitimacy of the use of force. But this is not sufficient. To understand its outcomes one needs to understand the reasons for social action and the meaning of the structural context in which a revolutionary movement develops.

Why didn't the *Sa-il-gu* uprising develop into a social revolution? Those who study the difference between a revolt and revolution point to the extent of demographic participation and the organizational strength of the contenders for power and the institutional strength of the state. The more people—especially the dominant sector—participate in the revolt, the more revolutionary the movement becomes. At the same time, the more social forces are institutionally organized, the more revolutionary the movement becomes. In fact revolution belongs to those who command organizational power.

For instance, in agrarian societies, "no peasant insurrections, no revolution" (Skocpol 1979:112-117). The Korean peasants, most of them beneficiaries of the 1948-1950 land reform, remained as they have been for many centuries, separated from each other in semi-isolated villages. An organized peasantry did not exist. Neither did the landed class exist since the land reform became a viable collective institution.

In addition to the university, mass media and political parties, the Korean military had developed since the war into a major institution. The armed forces grew from a meagre constabulary of 114,000, an army without a single tank," in 1949 into, "the fourth largest army of the free world with modern heavy equipment," numbering approximately 600,000 men in 1960. (Lee 1965:59). It was inevitable that , since 1963, the Korean military with its claim for speciality and qualification for defending the nation, would intervene in postrevolutionary chaotic politics to establish its own rule.

The point is that one cannot gauge a revolutionary situation by the structural yardsticks such as multiple sovereignty and "catnet." A revolutionary situation is the exchange of the violence and coercion between protesters and authority. The scale, quality and legitimacy of the interaction changes over time and varies from government to government. Our task then is to identify historically and comparatively the factors that institutionalize the power of social forces in such a way as to deinstitutionalize the power of authority at each stages of the revolutionary movement.

The Role of Political Exiles in Democratic Transitions: The Case of the Philippines

YOSSI SHAIN*

and

MARK THOMPSON**

ABSTRACT

Based on personal interviews (all conducted by Mark Thompson) and secondary sources, this essay examines the role of U.S.-based Filipino opposition in the struggle for democratic transition in the Philippines since 1972. The authors take a theoretical and comparative approach in evaluating the function of anti-Marcos exiles in challenging the dictator's attempts to consolidate his regime, and in contesting Marcos's legitimacy abroad. In conclusion, the authors offer some suggestive observations for further studies regarding the contribution of exiled dissidents to the unfolding of democratic regime changes.

THROUGHOUT THIS CENTURY political exiles have played an important role in the struggle against dictatorships and in the development of stable democracies. Exile groups contributed significantly in instances where the impulse for a democratic change came primarily from within their native country, and were also instrumental in cases where democratization was mainly the result of foreign countries' intervention.

After the end of the Second World War, exile groups were crucial to the installation of post-war democracies in Western Europe. In their uncompromising resistance to the Nazis, exile groups contributed to the defeat of their home countries' regimes—foreign and native—and to the process of monitored installation of post-war democracies. Italian Anti-Fascist exiles, known as fuorusciti, laid the foundations for the domestic resistance to Mussolini. From their European and U.S. bases, members of *Giustizia e Liberta* and of the exiled Socialist and Communist parties played a key role in injecting life into the underground opposition. In 1943, the Italian exiles reunited with their countrymen to take part in the final phase of Italy's redemocratization, and later acquired important posts in the new "party directories, ministries and the Constituent Assembly" (Delzell, 1961: 45). De Gaulle's exile

* Department of Political Science, Tel Aviv University, Ramat Aviv, Israel.
** Department of Political Science, Yale University, New Haven, Connecticut 06520-3532, U.S.A.

organization, the Free French, founded in London in opposition to Vichy's capitulation to the Nazis, gradually developed from an enterprise of a self-imposed exile, who proclaimed himself to be "the leader of all Frenchmen," to a recognized provisional government which was eventually to become the democratic foundations of liberated France. Likewise, the governments-in-exile of Norway and the Benelux countries were natural successors to their countries' occupiers, and helped to resume a swift normal democratic process. The exiled governments "became symbols of national unity and of resistance to the invader; the resistance movement did not challenge [their] legitimacy, ... and the conquerors did not succeed in imposing any enduring socio-economic changes" (Stepan in O'Donnell et al. vol. 3, 1986: 66).

Since the late 1940s most democratic transitions of authoritarian regimes in Southern Europe, Latin America and recently in East Asia have been motivated and shaped by socio-political factors within the state. Here too, many exile groups were instrumental in the success of the opposition to bring a democratic change. The most notable example is the contribution of the exiled leadership of Acción Democrática to the downfall of Marcos Pérez Jiménez's dictatorship and to the 1958 redemocratization of Venezuela (Ameringer, 1974; Coppedge, 1988). Similarly, Colombia's 1957/8 democratic settlement could not have been achieved without the endorsement of the Conservative exiled leader Laureano Gómez. Despite strong objections from his domestic followers, Gómez worked from his exile in Spain to reach a compromise with his political rivals in the Liberal party, known as the Pact of Sitges, which eventually insured Colombia's redemocratization (Burton and Higley, 1987). In the last two decades exiles were also part of the struggle for democratic change in Chile, Argentina, Brazil and South Korea. In collaboration with the domestic opposition in their respective countries and through their campaigns in the international sphere these political exiles were able to contribute to the weakening of authoritarian regimes and to the strengthening of conditions for democratization (Angell and Carstairs, 1987; Graham-Yooll, 1987; D'Souza, 1987; Lee, 1987).

Yet to date, and despite the widespread interest in democratic regime change in recent years, the scholarly literature seldom mentions the role of the opposition from abroad, let alone systematically analyzing the contribution of exiled opposition to the unfolding of democratic transitions. This essay is a preliminary effort to close this gap. By examining the contribution of Filipino exiles to the breakdown of Ferdinand Marcos's dictatorship, we seek to provide some general observations about the ways through which exile political activity may enhance the process of democratic regime change.

The Opposition to Marcos's Regime

Four major groups opposed the Marcos regime—democrats, communists, Muslim secessionists and military rebels—each advocating a different form of polity. The democratic opposition, our prime concern, advocated a pluralist constitutional government; the communists promoted a revolutionary authoritarian regime; the secessionists struggled for a separate Muslim state; and the dissident soldiers favored a military junta.[1] With the exeption of the military rebels, all these groups had operational bases abroad.

The umbrella organization of the communist opposition to Marcos, the National Democratic Front (NDF), had an exile office in Holland. Headed by the former priest Luis Jalandoni, the NDF developed a wide network of foreign support, especially among Scandinavian labor groups, which provided financial assistance to the communist domestic struggle. To date, the exile communists continue to pose a threat to the government of Corazon Aquino who in 1987 asked the Dutch authorities to monitor Jalandoni's revolutionary activities (Clad, 1987: 40-42).

In the late 1960s, in an attempt to counter a plan by the Manila government to conquer Sabah, the Malaysian government began training young Muslim-Filipino rebels, who in 1971 founded the Moro National Liberation Front (MNLF). When as a result of the declaration of martial law in September 1972, heavy fighting broke out between Muslim rebels and the Philippine government, the MNLF won the patronage of Muammar Gaddaffi, who in the spirit of "Islamic solidarity" provided sanctuary to the MNLF leader, Nur Misuari, and supplied the organization with arms, ammunition and equiptment (Noble, 1987).

The Democratic Forces

The imposition of authoritarian rule is always followed by various degrees of repression against potential and active opponents. In an attempt to create a climate of fear and submissiveness, authoritarian regimes use intimidation, detention, arrests, forced exile, kidnapping, assassinations and other measures to eliminate, suppress and co-opt its opponents. With the growing deterioration of the domestic forces of opposition, political exiles often assume a greater role in resisting the regime's hegemony. As a student of South African politics observed, in times of domestic repression the terrain of exile "can provide protection, security, powerful forms of external support, factors and conditions which facilitate the development of a form and quality of organization unattainable in the precarious circumstances of opposition politics within the homeland" (Lodge, 1987: 2-3).

The declaration of martial law in September, 1972 largely demobilized the democratic forces inside the Philippines. With congress abolished, the press shackled, and key opposition leaders imprisoned, the opposition Liberal Party lost its national forum for criticizing Marcos. Patronage-dependent mayors and governors, who now could be replaced by Marcos, were compelled to make their peace with the new political order, and *ad hoc* groups of politicians and social activists with the informal backing of the Catholic Church could muster only limited support in an attempt to boycott Marcos's self-legitimizing plebiscites. With domestic opposition virtually silenced, exiles in the United States emerged as the most active moderate anti Marcos group.

Just a day before the imposition of martial law, former senator Raul Manglapus left the Philippines for a speaking engagement in the U.S., thus escaping an arrest order. Upon his arrival in the U.S., Manglapus tried to convince Carlos Romulo, a famous journalist, former army general, and then the Philippines' Ambassador to the U.N., to lead an exile anti-Marcos movement. Romulo refused, choosing instead to return home to serve as Marco's Minister of Foreign Affairs. (Manglapus, 1987: xvi). In 1973, after smuggling his family out of the country, Manglapus founded the Movement for a Free Philippines (MFP), the first democratic exile organization to challenge Marcos. Manglapus prided himself on being part of a long tradition of Filipino exiles struggling for the liberation of their country. When in 1987 Manglapus delivered the annual Jose Rizal Memorial Lecture to the Poets, Essayists, and Novelists (PEN) Conference at the Cultural Center of the Philippines, he recalled how he was inspired by the struggle of Filipino exiles to free their country from Spanish colonial rule: ''In our years of exile, we presumptuously compared our appeals in Washington to those of Rizal in Madrid, drawing parallels for our success, failures, internal dissension, and methods of survival with those of the [old exiles]'' (reprinted in *Mr. & Ms.*, 5-11 June, 1987: 12).

Throughout the 1970s Manglapus was the key figure in the MFP. He was the Chairman of the Christian Social Movement (CSM)—the leading democratic left group founded in the mid-60s—which provided him with a wide organizational network inside the Philippines.[2] Manglapus was also related by marriage to one of the richest families in the Philippines, the Lopezes, who had become Marcos's *bête noire* after Vice-President Fernando Lopez joined the opposition in 1970. Fearing Marcos's rumored intention to declare martial law, Eugenio Lopez, the Vice-President's brother, and the family patriarch, went into self-imposed exile in the U.S. in mid-1972. A few months later, with military rule already in place, the Lopez family's financial holdings were seized and Eugenio Lopez, Jr., the Vice-President's nephew, was arrested. With his son held hostage Eugenio Lopez was forced to confront Marcos indirectly. He helped fund Manglapus's MFP and provided the organization with favorable publicity in the family-owned U.S. based newspaper, *The Philippine News*.

With few active members, the MFP activities were carried out by a core group in Washington D.C. which aside from Manglapus included Constitutional Convention delegate Heherson Alvarez, former Congressman Raul Daza, businessman Steve Psinakis, and student leader Charles Avila. This leadership was bolstered by several prominent exiles—Constitutional Convention delegate and now Congressman Bonifacio Gillego, Eugenio Lopez, Jr., who fled prison and arrived in the U.S. in 1977, and businessman Gaston Ortigas who escaped imprisonment before reaching the U.S. in 1980. The arrival of Benigno Aquino, Jr. in 1980 rejuvenated the U.S.-based opposition, although Aquino did not accept the MFP leadership.

International Campaigns and Diaspora's Support

In their quest for international sympathy and assistance political exiles are more likely to attract the support of enemies of their home regime, than to mobilize the home regime's allies on their behalf. After the Castro revolution, for example, the U.S. encouraged Cuban refugees to establish themselves as an exile opposition in accordance with an American plan to later employ them in the Bay of Pigs fiasco (Wyden, 1979). Governments friendly to the regime at home, however, tend to ignore the exiles' pleas and may even help their allies in suppressing exile activities under their jurisdiction. Such was the case of the C.I.A. assistance in the repression of anti-Shah Iranian exiles in the U.S. by agents of the Iranian secret police (SAVAK) (Garvey, 1980: 81).

In order to sway the allegiance of the home regime's allies, exiles must find indirect access to high governmental authorities usually through the manipulation of civil society agencies. They work to attract media attention to the home regime's atrocities, establish contacts with elected representatives and opinion makers, and try to convince cultural and sport associations to boycott international conferences in their country. An important strategy through which exiles may stir public opinion and contest the home regime's legitimacy is the mobilization of support among their fellow nationals abroad, including political refugees, overseas students and economic migrants. The diaspora community may assist the exiles morally and economically and sometimes succeed in shaping the policies of their countries of residence—especially if they are naturalized citizens— in favor of the exiles' struggle for democracy (Shain, 1989).

In the case of the Philippines, the exile MFP used all possible avenues to undermine the bond between Marcos and the U.S. Their activity was later consciously imitated by U.S.-based Korean opposition to the government of Chun Doo Hwan (Tolchin, 1986). While Muslim secessionists launched armed attacks across the borders and raised funds overseas, the democratic opposition abroad focused primarily on repudiating Marco's record in the U.S. through non-violent means. The MFP sought to convince U.S. officials to reduce—if not halt completely—military aid to the dictatorship, hoping that without such support the military would turn its back on Marcos. To achieve this goal Manglapus undertook a one-man propaganda campaign, testifying before Congress, writing opinion columns in major newspapers, appearing on television programs, and giving frequent speeches to Filipino Americans. Manglapus's activities were regularly reported in *The Philippine News*.

In June 1975 and May 1976 Manglapus attacked the Philippine government's human rights record before a special House subcommittee (cited in Manglapus, 1987: 70-71). In *The New York Times* (19 May, 1973; 4 Oct., 1973) and *The Washington Post* (2 Aug., 1977) he denounced Marco's regime as a ruthless dictatorship undeserving of U.S. assistance. On the popular television program, the "Today Show", he discounted the need for martial law, accused Marcos of human rights violations, and charged him of holding sham referendums to justify his rule (reproduced in Manglapus, 1987: 30-31). Another publicity coup in 1975 took place when Philippine media czar and a government insider, Primitivo Mijares, defected to the exile forces while on a trip to the U.S., and later made embarrassing revelations in his testimony before the House International Relations Subcommittee. Even more damaging to Marcos was the revelation, by columnist Jack Anderson, that Mijares had been offered a $50,000 bribe by Marcos for abstaining from testifying (*Washington Post*, 2 July, 1975). Another embarrassing episode took place when Napoleon Lechoco, a Filipino-American and an outspoken opponent of the regime in Manila, held the Philippine Ambassador to the U.S. hostage demanding Marcos allow his family to leave the Philippines. Lechoco charged that his family was used as a bargaining chip to force him to refrain from anti-Marcos activities. In 1977 he was acquitted in a U.S. court largely due to testimony by Manglapus, Psinakis and other prominent exiles, who portrayed in court the gloomy conditions under martial law, and diverted the public attention from the original accusation to the crusade for Philippine democracy (Psinakis, 1980: 59-60). When in April, 1980 Marcos came to the U.S. to attend the convention of the American Newspaper Publisher's Association (ANPA), MFP leaders held a counter forum in an adjacent room where they harshly denounced the Manila regime. The ANPA extended a last-minute invitation to Manglapus to address its gathering and the exile leader seized the opportunity to deliver a speech which was far better received than Marcos's rambling remarks and was later acclaimed by the association "as the most outstanding presentation by any speaker." *The Philippine News* reported that Marcos "was so infuriated by the Manglapus speech that he hastily called a press conference ... but the convention had ended and very few publishers were able to attend" (cited in Manglapus, 1987: 200).

The MFP campaign was clearly effective. An advocate of martial law, Filipino-American labor leader, Andy Mutan, reported to Marcos that the MFP was "destroying the image of the Philippine government in the U.S." (*Sunday Express*, 23 Sept., 1979). Robert Pringle, an American specialist on Southeast Asia, wrote, in 1980, that Marcos's poor reputation in Washington was largely due to the activity of anti-Marcos Filipino exile groups who exert "pressure on Congress out of proportion to their numbers" (Pringle, 1980: 57). A 1983 *Congressional Research Brief* reaffirmed that the exiles' "lobbying efforts in the U.S. have contributed to a call for a review of Philippine relations by some members of Congress" (Issue Brief, No. IB82102, 26 May, 1983).

Alarmed by the exiles' ability to provoke and channel international animosity toward his regime, Marcos moved to suppress the dissident forces abroad. In 1979 Mike Glennon, the counsel of the Senate Committee on Governmental Affairs reported in a classified report that as early as October 1973 the C.I.A. had become aware "that the Philippine government had become increasingly concerned that President Marcos's enemies in the U.S. might be developing, or had already, an influence that would adversely affect the Philippine government." The report added that since 1973 Gen. Fabian

Ver, Marcos's longtime bodyguard and later his Chief of Staff and Intelligence, began sending intelligence officers to the U.S. "for the purpose of infiltrating, monitoring and possibly counteracting the threat of anti-Marcos groups" (Poole and Vanzi, 1984b: 577-8). Moreover, in retaliation for his damaging congressional testimony, Mijares was apparently lured out of the U.S. and brought to the Philippines where his son was killed before his eyes and he was then tortured and murdered (Seagrave, 1988: 149). Assassination attempts were also made against Manglapus and other leading exiles, while other dissidents and their Filipino-American supporters underwent surveillance and experienced threats, financial blackmail and other forms of intimidation. These tactics were not without success. Fearing reprisals from Marcos's agents in the U.S. and concerned for their relatives inside the Philippines, many anti-Marcos Filippino-Americans abstained from joining MFP activities (Garvey, 1980; Poole and Vanzi: 1984a: 299).

Taking up "Terrorism"

Political exiles are often frustrated by their inability to undermine the regime at home by peaceful propaganda campaigns. Removed from the developments at home, and fearful that they will be forgotten, they may advocate violent and insurrectionary methods to overthrow the home regime. However, the domestic opposition which has to execute the exiles' violent strategy and bear the brunt of the government's retaliation, may decline to follow the exiles' advice, and may even blame the exiles for preferring to lead a comfortable life abroad while the insiders risk their lives (Edinger, 1956: 257). In the struggle against Marcos Perez Jimenez in Venezuela, for example, those who remained active in the resistance at home grew hostile to the leadership abroad and "considered the exiles cowards or fairweather friends for staying safely out of the country while the leaders of the underground were risking their lives daily" (Coppedge, 1988: 225). In Chile, too, the disinclination of the Communist domestic forces to follow the call of exiled Party leaders in Moscow to resort to violent resistance against Pinochet, eroded the exiles' prestige (Valenzuela and Valenzuela, 1986: 212).

Despite some successes in their propaganda campaign, by 1979 the democratic opposition to Marcos had become frustrated by the continuing stability of the Marcos regime. The hopes of the democratic forces has been raised by the revival of legislative elections in April 1978, and by the Carter Administration's declared human rights policy. But the legislative election, the first since the imposition of martial law, was so fraudulent that the opposition won only a few token seats in outlying provinces. Nonetheless, once he secured a new agreement on the U.S. military bases in Manila (January 1979) Jimmy Carter was quick to shelve criticism of Marcos, and the Manila government seemed to benefit from its repressive policies. The opposition desperately needed to 'raise the costs' for the dictatorship, and it was in this context that the democratic forces decided to resort to terrorist attacks against the Manila regime, a plan which was apparently first formulated by the exiles in the U.S.

In early 1978, Eduardo Olaguer, publisher of the Philippines' premier business newspaper *Business Day* and a man closely linked to anti-Marcos forces, traveled to the U.S. to raise funds for the Manila-based opposition. Olaguer who met with exile leaders later recalled Manglapus asking him: "Have you in Manila accepted the idea of armed struggle?" According to Olaguer, the exiles wished to demonstrate that they were more than "armchair revolutionaries" (interview with Olaguer, Metro Manila, March 17, 1987).

The exile leaders and Olaguer drew up a plan named "Operation Public Justice" which called for attacks on government personnel and property. When Olaguer returned to the Philippines with the proposal, domestic opposition leaders insisted on targeting only property. Consequently, Olaguer founded the "Light-a-Fire Movement" which burned down several government buildings in Manila. The exiles were instrumental in the activity of the Light-a-Fire Movement by providing the group with military-style training in the Arizona desert, and with some of the necessary explosives. But these attacks failed to produce the desired results. Marcos was able to minimize international publicity and exploit domestic criticism to undermine the opposition "terrorists." The capture of Filipino-American Ben Lim who was charged with smuggling explosives into the Philippines in December 1979, led to a government crackdown and the arrest of Olaguer and other Light-a-Fire activists (Psinakis, 1980: 11). Documents in their possession implicated the exile MFP and in late 1980 Manglapus was tried *in absentia* (Ocampo, 1980).

The experience of the Light-a-Fire Movement precipitated a debate among the exile dissidents. Steve Psinakis argued that a more successful campaign required other sophisticated explosives. Raul Manglapus and other exiles began questioning the wisdom of using violence before the opposition had time to establish a wider base of support at home. Benigno Aquino, Jr. stepped into the debate in May 1980. A leading opposition figure even before martial law, Aquino's stature was further enhanced after spending nearly eight years as Marcos's prisoner, before he was released to undergo heart surgery in the U.S. Before his departure Aquino promised Marcos to refrain from criticizing the regime while abroad. Shortly after his arrival, however, he broke his promise arguing that, "a pact with the devil, is no pact at all" (Neher, 1981: 266). In the U.S., Aquino became a research fellow at Harvard University, and according to Manglapus was immediately offered the leadership of the MFP (interview with Manglapus, Metro Manila, Nov. 20, 1986). Aquino refused. Instead he became part of the informal militant faction of the organization which included Steve Psinakis, Raul Daza, Heherson Alvarez and Charles Avila.

Behind the scenes Aquino and Psinakis collaborated in coordinating, training and arming a new terrorist group, the April 6 Liberation Movement (A6LM) named after the Manila opposition "noise barrage" which preceded the fraudulent elections of April, 1978. Like the Light-a-Fire, the A6LM sought to force the government to make political concessions and eventually to overthrow it all together. On August 4, 1980, in a speech before the Asia Society in New York, Aquino warned Marcos that he must reform his regime or face the consequences of urban violence:

"I have been told of plans for the launching of a massive urban guerrilla warfare where buildings will be blown up, and corrupt presidential cronies and cabinet members assassinated along with military officers who have engaged in wanton and rampant tortures of political prisoners. There are plans to disrupt tourism. Also to kidnap the children of corrupt aliens who have exploited our people mercilessly and who have profited immensely from their Palace connections. ...The guerrillas are well-educated, articulate young men and women who have patiently studied the latest tactics in urban warfare. If there is such a thing as the Light-a-Fire Movement, let me assure Mr. Marcos it will not be the last. More are coming, better-trained and better-prepared.... This is no idle talk. And Mr. Marcos would be well-advised to take this warning very seriously. He will soon face an opposition group distinct from the old politicians whom he has known and who have limited their dissent to mere rhetoric" (cited in Neher, 1981: 264).

In the months that followed, one person was killed and at least sixty others were injured in a series of bombings which attracted wide attention in the foreign media (Psinakis, 1980: 10). By 1981, however, a government crackdown led to the arrests of most A6LM members with others being forced into hiding. Aquino's "alleged involvement in and encouragement of bombing attacks have raised questions among moderates [at home] about him as a future leader" (Neher 1981: 268). Another activist group, the *Partido Demokratico-Sosyalista ng Pilipinas* (PDSP) and their exile bakers also began to build an army in Sabah, in collaboration with the Muslim secessionists of the MNLF, to wage guerrilla warfare against the Manila goverment. To arrange this alliance Benigno Aquino, Jr. met in August 1980 and again in May 1981 with MNLF exile leader Nur Misuari (Tasker, 1981: 20-22). Philippine government thwarted this joint project of the democratic exiles with the Muslim rebels.

Marcos used the bombing to convince the Reagan administration to crack down on anti-Marcos dissidents in the U.S. In March 1981 F.B.I agents began investigating prominent exile dissidents, including Ninoy Aquino and Steve Psinakis, whose house was raided. Other exile leaders, Charles Avila and Bonifacio Gillego, fled to Canada fearing arrest and eventual extradition. In late 1981, the Reagan administration introduced an extradition treaty with Marcos, but it was never passed in the U.S. Senate (Nations, 1982: 18). The American administration also used a provision in the "neutrality act" to launch a grand jury investigation into the activities of the exile opposition, which led to the indictment of Steve Psinakis and Charles Avila. In July 1987, more than a year after the fall of Marcos, Psinakis, on a visit to the U.S., was arrested in San Francisco, and was charged with attempting to smuggle explosives to the Philippines during "a period of violent opposition to Marcos" (Clad, 1987: 10-11). On April 6, 1988, Steve Psinakis filed a motion through his lawyers to dismiss the indictment against his alleged criminal activities. He accused the Reagan administration of double standards and hypocrisy in dealing with political exiles:

"The United States government, at the request of Philippine dictator Ferdinand Marcos, targeted for investigation and prosecution the leaders of the U.S.-based movement to restore democracy to the Philippines. The government did so at the same time that it was not only tolerating but actively supporting the actions of private groups in the United States to provide arms to the Nicaraguan Contras, and other Foreign resistance movements. Congressional investigation of the Iran-Contra affair, ...make it clear that whether ...a group supporting efforts in opposition to foreign government is encouraged, on the one hand or prosecuted on the other, depends on whether the group's political position is supported by the current administration" (*Philippine News*, 20-26 April, 1988: 12).

Growing Domestic Opposition and Exile Homecoming

The exiles' need to maintain a foothold at home increases when the home regimes moves toward liberalization. Gradual developments toward democracy are likely to shift the momentum of the struggle against the regime from the international to the national sphere, and to produce domestic leadership which may view the exile forces as anachronistic or even as a threat to the opening process. O'Donnell and Schmitter observed that "regime opponents, having been given virtually no role within the authoritarian scheme of governance and, in some cases, having returned from exile to act in societies which have undergone substantial changes, often have had to rely on precarious past identifies, outmoded slogans, and unimaginative combinations" (O'Donnell et al. vol. 4, 1986: 23).

Exile leaders who endeavour to perpetuate inside loyalties must keep in constant touch with developments at home. The timing of their homecoming is a critical factor in determining their role following the downfall of the home regime. Lenin's arrival at the Finland Station, for example, repersents a uniquely timed famous homecoming which eventually changed the course of history. On the other hand, exiled politicians who failed to return on time suffered marginality and encountered great obstacles in reintegrating themselves in the politics of their country. This happened during the redemocratization of Brazil, when in the early 1980s, returned exiles found themselves "strangers in their own country ... and were seen as intruders or competitors" (D'Souza, 1987: 207-8). Thus exiles who wish to join with their compatriots must find their way back home even if their return involves severe personal risk. Clodomiro Almeyda, former Foreign Minister in Allende's government, and since the 1973 coup the exiled leader of the Marxist wing of the Chilean Socialist party, made a dramatic return to Chile over the Andes in early 1987, to be immediately arrested by the Chilean police. In the midst of the Chilean opposition's campaign to unite forces in an attempt to overthrow Pinochet in the 1988 'yes'—'no' plebiscite, Almeyda, seeking a leading role in the internal development, ended his years in exile and returned to Chile to lead his supporters from a Santiago jail cell (Stepan, 1988: 34).

In January 1981 Marcos lifted marial law, while retaining the power to rule by decree. The limited political opening provided greater space for expressing dissent, and the government demonstrated greater tolerance toward labor strikes. The partial liberalization can be ascribed in part to Marcos's desire to make a favorable impression in the U.S. just days before Ronald Reagan was inaugurated as President, and also as an attempt to improve his international image before the visit of Pope John Paul to Manila in February, 1981. Many exiles, however, took credit for these domestic changes. They pointed to the activity of the Light-a-Fire Movement and the A6LM as instrumental in Marcos's decision to liberalize, and called attention to an earlier meeting between exiled leaders and Imelda Marcos in New York City, in which the U.S.-based opposition offered to call off violent attacks on the regime in exchange for political reforms.

With the gradual opening, and while domestic opposition groups worked to take advantage of the new political climate, the U.S.-based opposition saw the need to move closer to the forces in Manila. At home, the first mission of the moderate groups was to reorganize and unite forces in order to become a viable alternative to the regime. In 1982, a coalition of twelve opposition groups, including the U.S.-based opposition, announced the formation of the United Nationalist Democratic Organization (UNIDO) "to 'undo' the Marcos dictatorship and restore the fundamental institutions of democracy" (Youngblood, 1983: 215n). Although Aquino and Manglapus were both made Vice Presidents of UNIDO in charge of external operations and foreign affairs respectively, the domestic leadership had full control while the exiles' stature at home was declining. Moreover, Aquino and Manglapus both lost political influence when their respective political parties in the Philippines joined forces in 1982 and left UNIDO (*Mr. & Ms.* 30 Sept. 1983: 20). In 1981 Manglapus helped form and raised foreign funding for the *Partido Demokratikong Pilipino* (Philippine Democratic Party, PDP) largely made up of former members of his Christian Social Movement. While in prison, Aquino was behind the formation of *Lakas ng Bayan* (Strength of the People, LABAN) intended to challenge Marcos in Manila in the 1978 legislative elections. Despite their objection to the merger between their respective parties, Aquino and Manglapus remained powerless in the face of their domestic followers' determination to unite their forces, and were further humiliated when the new grouping asked them both to reapply for membership (interview with Bonifacio Gillego, Metro Manila, 24 Feb., 1987).

Fearing for his political future, Aquino decided in 1983 to return to Manila despite Marcos's attempts to convince him to stay abroad. In a phone conversation shortly before his departure, Ninoy Aquino maintained that Imelda Marcos, on her visit to New York on May 21, 1983, offered him a huge bribe to stay in Boston. She warned him that "the Marcoses might not be able to control their own people if he came home and that his life might be in danger" (Overholt, 1986: 1156). Ignoring Marcos's explicit threat, Aquino calculated that he would only be imprisoned, a preferable situation to the growing sterility of exile politics. But imprisonment was not the solution that the regime had in mind. On August 21, 1983 Aquino was gunned down as he stepped off the plane upon his arrival in Manila. The ruthless assassination provoked massive domestic opposition and a worldwide uproar.

Ironically, Aquino's assassination seemed to make other exiles' return more imperative and probably less dangerous. Many dissidents abroad, eager to join the growing domestic protest movement, assumed that Marcos would be hesitant to take harsh repressive measures against them. The next exiled leader to return home was Jovito Salonga. A former Senator (and now Senate president), Salonga was implicated and imprisoned for his alleged role in the A6LM bombings, before he went into exile in March, 1981. While in the U.S. Salonga spent most of his time drafting a new platform for the Liberal Party and investigating Marcos's hidden wealth abroad. His homecoming in January, 1985 coincided with rumors that Marcos would soon call a 'snap' presidential election, and Salonga planned to challenge the regime (Sacerdoti, 1985). Several months later, Salonga's ally Raul Daza ended twelve years of exile and returned to Manila despite pending charges that implicated him in the A6LM bombing campaign. Unable to get the charges dropped and facing the prospect of a lengthy trial ahead, Daza left the country a few months later. (*Malaya Magazine*, 29 Dec., 1985: 1).

The Aquino assassination, although further shifting the momentum of the struggle against Marcos from the international stage to the home front, was by no means the kiss of death to the exiles' campaign abroad. The Filippino exiles now enjoyed greater access to U.S. government officials and elected representatives who were increasingly becoming disenchanted with Marcos's human rights record, and thus more attentive to the exiles' appeal. An October, 1983 Newsletter, published by The Movement for a Free Philippines, listed 86 U.S. Congressional allies of the opposition to the government in Manila (MFP Newsletter Oct. 1983: 3).

The exiled democratic forces were now divided between the MFP and the newly-formed Ninoy Aquino Movement (NAM) headed by Heherson Alvarez, Aquino's ally in exile. The two groups joined with left-wing exile organizations, including the Campaign Against the Marcos Dictatorship (CAMD) and the Church Coalition for Human Rights, in lobbying on Capitol Hill. They urged the U.S. Congress to halt or at least to reduce military aid to Marcos, and publicized the human rights abuses of the regime. Although the exiles were unable to convince Congress to reduce military aid to Marcos, their efforts were by no means futile. In May, 1984 a sizable minority of U.S. House members supported a notion which advocated full suspension of military aid to the Philippines, and the exiles interpreted the vote as a meaningful shift in their direction (MFP Newsletter, Feb. 1985: 7). At this late phase of Marcos's rule the exiles further served the cause of domestic opposition by providing incriminating materials against the regime. The MFP executive director, Bonifacio Gillego, provided the initial research for a *Washington Post* article which exposed Marcos's fraudulent claim to be a WW II hero. When a Manila opposition newspaper, *We Forum* reprinted Gillego's story it was quickly shut down. The exiles also tipped off American journalists about Marcos's hidden wealth in the U.S. which led Filippino oppositionists in parliament to initiate impeachment proceedings against the president (*Malaya Magazine*, 9 Sept., 1985).

A week after her husband's assassination, Corazon Aquino returned from the U.S. She described her years as exile-housewife in Boston as the happiest time of her life (Komisar, 1987: 45). Although she was not politically minded before her return to Manila, Corazon Aquino immediately became an important symbol as the martyr's widow, and when Marcos announced a 'snap' presidential election for February 1986, the democratic forces turned to her as the only person who could unite their ranks and the Filippine people behind them. As a fall-back in the likely event that the balloting would be rigged, Corazon Aquino's advisers conducted secret discussions with some dissident soldiers in the Reform the Armed Forces Movement (RAM) who were contemplating a coup following the election (Simons, 1987: 266-8). At the same time, exile MFP leaders openly courted RAM members then training in the U.S. to join their anti-Marcos campaign. At least seven members of RAM in the U.S. defected to the exile forces shortly before the elections (*Malaya Magazine*, 20 March, 1986). The MFP and the dissident soldiers conspired to help overthrow Marcos in case the election proved fraudulent, but this proved unnecessary since the regime was toppled in a spontaneous uprising after a failed coup attempt.

The peaceful transition of power closely matched the prescription of Manglapus in his twelve-country study of redemocratization. In a 1985 paper the exile leader argued that in order to succeed the opposition had to pursue electoral struggle, hold demonstrations, receive the backing of the Catholic Church and win over the military. By allying themselves with the RAM the exile MFP helped strengthen the relations between civilian and soldier dissidents.

Manglapus considered a homecoming before the 1986 election, but was deterred by subversion charges pending against him. When he finally returned after the February revolution he received a hero's welcome from Aquino's newly-established government, although many anti-Marcos dissidents questioned his delayed homecoming. Under Corazon Aquino many prominent exiles were rewarded with government positions and presidential support. Heherson Alvarez was appointed Minister of Agrarian Reform in the provisional government, and in the 1987 congressional election Alvarez and Manglapus were chosen as administration candidates for the Senate while Raul Daza and Bonifacio Gillego were backed in their bid for seats in the lower house. They all won. Raul Manglapus later became Foreign Secretary, Salonga was elected senator and then became President of the Senate, Charles Avila was elected mayor of the municipality of Tanauan, and the Lopez family recovered most of its financial holdings.

Conclusion

This essay has examined the contribution of Filipino opposition abroad to the erosion of Marcos's regime and to its eventual replacement by a democratic system. In conclusion we will evaluate the case in an attempt to further elaborate on the role of the exiled opposition in democratic transitions. As demonstrated above, the U.S.-based Filipino opposition helped perform a variety of functions which Alfred Stepan has listed critical to the success of all opposition forces seeking democratization (Stepan, 1980). The Filipino exiles were instrumental in the struggle of the moderate forces to "resist integration;" that is, to skillfully challenge the regime's attempts to eliminate, suppress, demobilize or coopt its opposition; they played a key role in contesting Marcos's international legitimacy; and contributed significantly to the process of "raising the cost of authoritarian rule" as well as to the "creation of a democratic alternative."

According to Stepan, in order to resist integration, democratic opposition forces must maintain an autonomous and viable organization "even if only from exile" to infuse life among passive opponents of the regime. By and large, the more succesful a regime is in imposing its hegemonic rule, the greater the likelihood that political exiles will assume a greater role in resisting integration. In fact in most cases the emergence of exile opposition groups is in itself an indication of the increasing difficulty in challenging the regime from within. The imposition of Mussolini's dictatorship in November 1926, for example, led to the establishment of exile anti-Fascist groups in Europe which for years shouldered the struggle against the Duce and contested his claims to enjoy the unanimous support of the Italian people (Delzell, 1961). In Nazi Germany, where many segments of the population were reconciled to the regime, and where resistance groups were atomized and ruthlessly suppressed, anti-Nazi exile opposition groups remained the sole spokesmen of the "other Germany" (Edinger, 1956). Likewise, under Trujillo's repressive dictatorship in the Dominican Republic, "the only opposition parties were organized in exile" (Ameringer, 1974: 46).

Naturally the role of exile opposition in resisting integration is potentially greater under political systems which practice absolute intolerance to any form of dissent than under dictatorships such as Marcos's which permit some pluralism and tolerate limited non-violent opposition. Under the latter kind of authoritarian regime, the respective roles of the internal opposition and the exiled dissidents are often interrelated and complementary. In Venezuela, for example, as long as the domestic opposition remained viable the activity of the exiled Acción Democrática was subsidiary and was designed to abet the internal struggle. However, when the home front was passive the forces abroad took the lead in resisting integration by exploiting their relative freedom to contest the regime's legitimacy in the international arena (Ameringer, 1974: 159).

Although the Manila government was significantly less repressive than many other authoritarian regimes, the activity of the Filipino exile opposition was nonetheless critical in resisting integration during the early period of martial law. In the 1970s, with the domestic opposition demobilized and partially integrated into the new authoritarian institutions, the MFP was one of the few voices raised against the regime. Alejandro Roces, former Secretary of Education and well-known journalist argued that the exiles "sustained the momentum of the assault on the dictatorship in the dark days" (*Midweek Magazine*, 16 April, 1986: 8). The exile leader Raul Daza maintained that "the MFP was the only organization which kept the fires burning during the early martial law days" (interviewed in Metro Manila, February 19, 1987).

Authoritarian governments which are usually confident of their ability to suppress domestic opposition, are often frustrated by their failure to control the activity of their opponents abroad. Operating from outside their country, and sometimes under the sanctuary of sympathetic governments, political exiles are in a unique position to discredit the regime's legitimacy and to expose its oppressive nature abroad. As Stepan points out, "the stronger the international repugnance, the more the costs of rule are raised" (Stepan, 1980: 17).

In the case of the Philippines, the exiles' vigorous campaign to expose human rights violations and to undermine Marcos's personal credibility in political and media circles in the U.S., thrust a wedge in Filipino-U.S. relations. In a final attempt to vindicate his reputation, the now deceased exiled dictator Ferdinand Marcos argued that the primary reason for the shift in the once-friendly U.S. posture toward his regime was "the contrived image of Philippine reality" implanted in the U.S. public opinion during the 1970s and the early 1980s "by the articulate and well-financed representatives of anti-Marcos expatriates residing in North America." Marcos added that "the representation made by anti-Marcos spokesmen in committee and subcommittee hearings in the United States Congress were given the widest circulation by the American press; [and that] the wildest charges [against him] were given credence" (Marcos, 1989).

Whether Marcos's image was distorted or accurately represented by Filippino exiles, the fact remains that the regime's attempt to repress dissidents in the U.S. further eroded Marcos's prestige. Marcos's anti-exile campaign in the U.S., like the assaults against Chilean exiles by Gen. Pinochet's DINA and against Iranian dissidents by the Shah's SAVAK, may have enjoyed tacit C.I.A. approval. However, the exposure of such atrocities often gravely damages friendly relations between the regime at home and the host country. Thus, for example, the brutal murder of former ambassador Orlando Letelier by DINA agents in the U.S., exposed Pinochet to heavy criticism and pressure from the Carter administration and other European democracies. Pinochet was forced to extradite Letelier's assassins to the U.S., to dissolve the DINA and to restrain its campaign against critics abroad (Garvey, 1980).

The case of the Philippines also exemplifies the accuracy of Robert Dahl's dictum that, "The likelihood that a government will tolerate an opposition increases as the expected costs of suppression increases" (cited in Stepan, 1980; 19). International criticism, generated in part by the exiles, was a major factor in Marcos's decision to lift martial law in 1981. Of no less importance was Marcos's desire to put an end to terrorist attacks in Manila, that were contemplated and directed by the leadership abroad.

For the most part, the liberalization of the domestic political scene is likely to shift the center of gravity away from the exiles to the internal-based opposition. However even at this juncture the exiles' role is by no means over. They may help to accelerate the regime's breakdown by perpetuating a two-front political assault on the home regime—domestic and international—but more important still, by helping in the formation of a unified and viable opposition alternative. As Stepan points out, a crucial task of the democratic opposition is to integrate as much of the anti-authoritarian movements as possible in order to counter the regime's claim to be "the only viable alternative" (Stepan, 1980: 20). Although the leadership of Ninoy Aquino and Manglapus was challenged to a degree by the formation of UNIDO, their endorsement of the new coalition helped solidify UNIDO as the most significant alternative to the regime.

Finally, in preferring a risky homecoming to political oblivion abroad, exile leaders may give a final boost to the opposition spirit, although sometimes at the cost of their own lives.

NOTES

1   This classification oversimplifies a more complex situation consisting of a multitude of overlapping opposition groups. This list consists only of contestants for *power* in the Philippines and does not include civil society agents such as the Catholic Church and the Labor Movement, despite their critical role in the anti-Marcos movement.
2   According to Dennis M. O'leary of the Filipino Information Service (1980), Manglapus's followers in the democratic left included 2.500 armed men and a mass base of one million potential supporters.

Islam, Culture and Revolution: The Case of Iran

BRIGID A. STARKEY*

ABSTRACT

Discussions of the Iranian Revolution and questions about why it took place when it did, and why it took place in the way that it did have proliferated in the past ten years in the discipline of political sciences. Theoretical focuses have ranged from those of the mobilization effects of charismatic leadership and revolution, in the Weberian tradition; to Marxist analyses of the relations of production in pre-revolutionary societies; and finally to the Durkheimian School's theories of "psychologism" in collective action. There has also been a tendency to treat the religious dimension of the revolution as determinative, and part of a monolithic process of political change. There is, however, one attribute of the revolution that remains constant in its abstract form through all of these various approaches, and that is the cultural dimension of the Iranian revolution. This paper attempts to develop a more coherent cultural framework from which to view the occurrences of 1978-1979.

The Transnational Islamic Movement and the Iranian Revolution

MOST INDEPTH ANALYSES of the contemporary transnationalist Islamic movement have cautiously pointed out that the movement is by no means monolithic and that causes, goals and projected outcomes vary by country; each a unique historical entity (Hunter, 1988). If one accepts this theory that a transnationalist Islamic impulse may exist, but that specific cases must be isolated and examined separately, then the qualifying question becomes whether Islam is being used to legitimize social unrest or whether it is generating the unrest itself on a case by case basis. This produces the dichotomous categories of Islam as either a tool of legitimation or of determination. It also provides the connection between cultural modes of analysis and the phenomenon of social revolution.

The inherent danger in the use of the term "Islamic fundamentalism" is that it refers to a demand for historical regression, a demand for a return to pre-modernization. If one uses this term for all Islamic movements, one is guilty of committing a reductionist fallacy, in that this trend is only present in some of the movements, but by no means all (Azar and Moon, 1983). Clearly in the Iranian case the revolutionary phenomenon must be seen as comprising two distinct phases. The first was the social movement culminating in the downfall of the Shah; the second was the replacement of the institution of the monarchy with a still-evolving Islamic state structure.

* Department of Government and Politics, The University of Maryland at College Park, College Park, Maryland 20742, U.S.A.

The political reality of the second phase calls into question the use of the concepts of fundamentalism and/or revivalism in the Iranian context. A more accurate description of the phenomenon can be found in the term "Islamization", which in the Iranian case referred to the dynamic process of redefining political realities based upon widely-accepted religious tenets. That is, as a cultural force Islam had never rescinded to the degree where we could now refer to its "rebirth" in Iranian society. The social change of the Iranian revolution was not premised on a return to the past, but rather on a new political future more firmly rooted in the Shi'i Islamic heritage of Iran, rather than the political status quo, so widely perceived as illegitimate within Iran.

The common denominator in the transnationalist Islamic movement is rooted in a common desire for social change. The desire for a social order premised on various tenets of Islam is pervasive, as is the proclaimed desire for realization of the "'umma" or transnational community of believers (Piscatori, 1986). So, while each Islamic movement is confronting a different political reality at home and expressing different political aspirations at the state level, the concepts of "fitna" for the Shi'is and "jihad" for the Sunnis are leading to common ends.[1] Specifically, political action in the name of Islam is no longer being explicitly aimed at wiping out the existence of an illegitimate state structure. Now the emphasis is on "Islamizing" the state and societal structures to make them legitimate (Piscatori, 1986). This is a crucial distinction that must be acknowledged as we look in depth at the role of Islam as a cultural force and as a political legitimizer in the evolution of the Iranian social revolution of 1978-79.

The Cultural Mode of Analysis

The work of Theda Skocpol has assumed a position of eminence in the study of social revolution over the past decade. Rooted firmly in the structuralist tradition, Skocpol's approach has been neo-Marxist, as evidenced by her definition of a social revolution as a rapid, basic transformation of a society's state and clas structures, accompanied and in part carried through by class-based revolts from below (Skocpol, 1979). While she adds to traditional Marxist analyses of revolution by emphasizing the role of the state rather than economic determinism exclusively, she nevertheless is primarily concerned with identifying external pressures on the internal dynamics of changing states.

While the state must be considered an important object of analysis in the Iranian case, more emphasis must be placed on culture as a specific level of analysis. This entails moving beyond the structural focus of the neo-state literature and concentrating on the latter force in Migdal's characterization of "strong societies, weak states" (Migdal, 1989). Specifically, the question must be asked: In what way is a society strong and why? The answer to this question involves developing the notion of culture as a political variable.

How to use culture as a variable in political analysis has long been a contentious question. No one has suggested dismissing it as a force that must be reckoned with, yet it is more often than not ignored because of its inhospitability to empirical scrutiny. The concept has most effectively been used in the social sciences by anthropologists, who have focused on its micro-level explanatory power in considerations of individuals' values and belief systems.

The main concern for political scientists in adapting the concept has been the connection of the micro to the macro. They have attempted to explain how whole societies connect to each other based on the premise of the sharing of these values and beliefs, and the socialization process that gives life to the political parameters of societies (Pye, 1972; Almond and Verba, 1980). Culture is, therefore, the glue which holds a society or subgroups within a society together. It is both the vehicle and the product of the search for intersubjective meanings. Douglas and Wildavsky refer to this end product as the "collective construct" which serves as the guiding thread as people look for rules into which a vision of the "good life" can be effectively translated (Douglas and Wildavsky, 1982). Bernard Lewis also employs the linguistic metaphor in his description of the "political language of Islam" (Lewis, 1988). And Reza Behnam sets the stage for the utility of the political culture concept in relation to contemporary Iran when he writes,

> The function of a culture system is to provide the rules, techniques, and understandings necessary for the continued survival of the group. Culture also forges a link between the values and behavior patterns of members of a political system and the form and action of government in that system. Political culture involves the fundamental collective understandings a society has about power, authority, and action. (Behnam, 1986: 9)

The inherent value of looking at social revolutions from within a cultural framework, therefore, is that culture as a level of analysis has dual utility. It is culture that lends meaning to political language in a given setting, and it is culture that also mobilizes political action in that same setting (Laitin, 1986). Juxtaposing these two faces of culture, as Laitin has referred to them, provides the analyst with the ability to explain how the search for intersubjective meanings propels socio-political change. Nowhere are the dynamics of this process more clear than in the contemporary Muslim world, and this study now turns specifically to Iran as a case in point.

Phase One of the Revolution: Islam as a Cultural Vehicle

The past decade has seen a lively debate among experts on Iran over the question of whether the Iranian revolution was an "Islamic revolution".[2] The main point of contention if one reads between the lines of this ongoing dialogue, is whether Islam is to be considered a religious or a cultural force, or whether the two can be seen as parts of a whole. The temptation to characterize events in Iran as part of an essentially religious phenomenon seems understandable in view of the end result: the Islamic Republic of Iran. The analyst, however, must separate the process itself from the results of the process. The "roots of revolution" run deep in the Iranian case and include economic displacement, political alienation and nationalist resentment (Keddie, 1981).

The lack of economic and political integration into the structure of a "modern Iran" was striking under the Shah. His resultant need to resort to coercion in order to enforce social order was undoubtedly an accelerator in its own right, in the movement toward collective mobilization. Economic changes which the Shah was pushing through in the name of reform were causing rapid displacement of the traditional sectors of the economy. Likewise, existing between the narrow elite and the masses in Iranian society, the growing middle class in Iran was suffering from political and cultural malaise, the result of being caught in the middle between established traditions and imported changes.

An even graver error on the Shah's part was his belief that enhanced internal legitimacy would come his way as a result of his significant position in the international security system. The Shah's increased military prowess was not perceived in the positive nationalist light in which he attempted to place it, but was rather once again seen as threatening through the cultural prism which had become the political guide of the Iranian people. The Shah's identification with the unpopular superpower tug-of-war, in which the Iranian people saw themselves as pawns, became a liability, rather than the source of legitimacy which he had hoped it would be. Secure and legitimate in the eyes of the West, the Shah's own people perceived themselves to be in an inferior and dependent position vis a vis the West (Sick, 1985; Bill, 1988).

There have been several attempts to characterize the Iranian revolution as being primarily economically motivated (Momayezi, 1986; Parsa, 1986). Yet there are logical contradictions in this approach, given the fact that the middle class had been growing and prospering under the Shah, and most importantly that the language of protest was never primarily an economic language. While economic frustration was undoubtedly real in the Iran of the 1970s, its primacy is extremely questionable if one attempts to assess the most important factors behind the movement. The economic frustration seems to have been more a part of the general frustration and social malaise that Iranians were feeling as result of their perceived weakness as active forces in their own destinies. Much has been written on the history of Iran as a history of a nation constantly being militarily and by extension, culturally, invaded by forces from the outside.[3] Anti-westernism, specifically anti-Americanism is the latest manifestation of this pervasive societal mindset. A very interesting extension to this characterization of Iranians as having a national image of themselves as the oppressed, the violated, the perennial "underdogs", is the parallel self-image that one finds in the Shi'i Islamic tradition (Irfani, 1983; Rajaee, 1989). Irfani (1983) and Rajaee (1989) have pointed to the notion of Shi'ism as being largely an Iranian interpretation of Islam. Therefore, a combination of the lending of Shi'i legitimacy to the underdog mentality, and the notion that Iranian Shi'ism is uniquely Iranian lend credence to a cultural interpretation of the intellectual force of Islam in the first revolutionary phase. The question of its revolutionary force is another question, however. Here we must emphasize, as Behnam does, that historically there was political inaction in the face of the perceived oppression. The Shi'i concept of *taqiyya*, which can be described as the practice of "quietly" and "non-confrontationally" practicing your faith was historically a widely-accepted tenet. Revolution (*thanatos*) was a secular notion with no precedence in Shi'i political language. The revolutionary impetus arose during a time when *taqiyya* was being replaced by *fitna*, the notion that a rebellion of the faithful against the oppressors was a moral obligation for good Muslims (Behnam, 1986).

It was in this environment that the powerful messages of modern Islamic intellectuals like Ali Shariati began to take hold. Shariati, in a series of influential lectures at Iranian universities in the 1970s, played hard and repeatedly on the following themes: the only way to political and social freedom lay within Iranian tradition, the "Iranian self". If Iranians were to free themselves from oppression, they would first have to find the correct ideology of liberation within their own beliefs and values. He rejected the foreign ideologies of Marxism, capitalism and nationalism. He believed that adherence to these only widened the gulf between the Iranian masses who were strongly attached to Islamic tradition, and the intellectuals who claimed to speak for Iran. Shariati feared an Iran in which intellectuals would become isolated from their own "cultural heritage" and would speak a language not understood to their own people (Irfani, 1983; Limbert, 1987). In response, Shariati constructed a vision of a new "self" for Iranian intellectuals, a self which would be based on a new dynamic version of Shi'ite Islam. A version that could become a political ideology, and an ideology of protest and change.

The question that must be asked then is whether Shariati and others like him were inciting a revolution or whether they were providing a theme around which widespread discontent could be channeled? The consideration of Islam as a cultural force, which is the theme of this paper, suggests support for the latter view. Specifically, Islam became a vehicle for the creation of the collective articulation of societal discontent, as well as the simultaneous mobilizer for political action vis-à-vis that discontent.

Islam became a synthesizer of cultural uniqueness and political action. In this way, it was largely the symbolic and organizational aspects, not the explicitly religious, which became unifying forces. Bernard Lewis has most eloquently captured the power of Islam in this regard,

> In political life, Islam ... offers the most widely intelligible formulation of ideas, on the one hand of social norms and laws, in the other, of new ideals and aspirations. And, as recent events have repeatedly demonstrated, Islam provides the most effective system of symbols for political mobilization... (Lewis, 1988: 5)

The Iranian revolution occurred as the result of the temporary convergence of a wide variety of groups and individuals who shared three common attributes: they were Iranians; they were Muslims; and they opposed the rule of Mohammed Reza Pahlavi. On the question of why Islam arose as the unifying force of identification, much can be learned from Laitin's description:

Very rarely do cultural systems coincide perfectly within a large society. People must often choose which religious group, language group, and so on will be their primary mode of cultural identification. This choice is often guided by instrumental reasoning, based on the potential resources available for identifying yourself...once a cultural group organizes politically, the common symbolic system makes for efficient collective action... not because culture is more real than class but because organizational costs are relatively low when common and powerful symbols are readily available and rules of exclusion easily formulated. (Laitin, 1988: 591)

One can look at the collective mobilization around Shi'i Islamic symbols in a similar light. Emphasis here must be on the already established communication network that the Mosques had with the people of Iran, as well as the close identification between pre-Pahlavi Iranian nationalism and Iranian Shi'ism. Three points seem salient in this regard.

Firstly, the Mosque was an entity that was economically independent of the state, and therefore endowed with an independent base. In Shi'i Islam, unlike Sunni Islam, the faithful pay their religious tax (*zakat*) and a further levy known as *khoms* directly to the Mosque. Secondly, Shi'i religious leaders (Ayatollahs Montazeri, Shariatmadari, Khomeini) were analogous to American folk heroes in the long national struggle against the Pahlavi monarchy. While numerous analysts have pointed to the significant co-optation of the relgious leadership into the Pahlavi regime, the fact remains nevertheless that the popular perception of the clergy was one of political opposition. Finally, rooted in the pre-Islamic history of Iran was a precedent for clerical intervention in the socio-political affairs of the country (Akhavi, 1985; Moshiri, 1985).

Both Keddie (1972) and Rajaee (1989) emphasize that the success of the ulama as the main revolutionary organizers (as opposed to secular opponents of the regime) came as a result of the ideological and political ties which they shared with the masses. Moreover, these ties cut across any class lines that existed in Iran. The appeal of a revolution rooted in a renaissance of Iranian uniqueness was nearly universal during the months of intense struggle with the Pahlavi regime. The role of Islam was clearly an instrumental one during this phase of the revolutionary process. This is illustrated in the empirically-based work of Shaul Bakhash on the mobilizational role of Islam during 1978 (Bakhash, 1984).

Bakhash, by examining sermon transcripts from Friday Mosque services, as well as the contents of revolutionary pamphlets, is able to tell a very interesting story about the "Islamization" of the anti-Shah movement in Iran. The first stage in the revolutionary process is described by Bakhash as the mass demonstrations that occurred in such cities as Qom, Mashad, Isfahan and Shiraz as demonstrators protested the crimes the Shah was committing against the people. All through 1978 these demonstrations occurred in city after city, and over the course of the year they began to coincide more frequently with religious occasions, or in support of religious figures. Step two was the articulation of the anti-Shah sentiments in the form of pamphlets that were distributed en masse to the people of Iran. Initially playing on the theme of the Shah as a lackey of corrupt western influences, the pamphlets became progressively more concentrated on totally discrediting the person of the Shah and any efforts at reform that he offered to make. Ultimately they became the vehicle for the notion that the exiled religious figure, the Ayatollah Khomeini, would return to establish the only workable alternative to the monarchy—an Islamic government.

Two interesting points about these revolutionary pamphlets stand out. Firstly, there were the Islamic overtones to the discreditation of the Shah and the future course for the movement to take, and secondly, there was the fact that these themes were being utilized even by secular leaders of the opposition movement. This reflects widespread realization of the notion that an effective medium had been found and was reaching the people of Iran. The Islamization of the movement became synonymous with both its radicalization and its enhanced unity.

The best indications that the religious element was being utilized more for its symbolic and cultural appeal than for its governmental possibilities comes in that (a) the notion of an Islamic state clearly evolved over time in the pamphlets and sermons (It was *not* the initial impetus of the Islamic theme in the overall social movement.) and (b) when the Khomeini leadership and the drive for an Islamic state came to fruition following the departure of the Shah and the events of the following several months, the revolutionary coalition came apart at the seams. Distress at the course that the revolution had taken was evident amongst many groups including the Islamic modernists, the communist elements, the Iranian equivalent of a bourgeoisie, many feminists, lay intellectuals, ethnic minorities and those with both stricter and looser interpretations of Shi'i Islamic precedent (Irfani, 1983; Hiro, 1985).

Phase Two of the Revolution: Islam and the State

The initial revolutionary coalition had used Islam in a distinctly legitimate and instrumental fashion. However, it was the success of the Islamic idiom during this first phase that seems to have led to its determinative role in the second phase: the establishment of an Islamic state.

First phase events in Iran seem to have qualified it as one of Skocpol's social revolutions. However, though this seems a suitable label when considering only that stage, the consolidation of the revolution, an on-going process, raises doubts about this description of events. The revolution was not essentially structural in that authoritarian rule remains the mode of government in Iran. In addition, there is no evidence that the class structure of Iranian society has seen a significant transformation in the post-revolutionary era. Rather, as Said Arjomand has written, the burden of explanation shifts, in the case of Iran, from standard structural explanations to the system of communication. This is where the essentially cultural mode of analysis adds a vital dimension to explanations of events in revolutionary Iran (Arjomand, 1984).

While the Islamic revolution does not seem to have significantly altered either the political or social structure of pre-revolutionary Iran, it has significantly altered the cultural milieu in which politics now takes place. Internal legitimacy coupled with external illegitimacy now color the political land-scape of the nation of Iran.

The most salient characteristic of the second phase of the revolution was the political role which the Ayatollah Khomeini defined for himself. As previously alluded to, the revolutionary coalition had included fudamentalists such as Khomeini, traditionalists, modernists and even some secularists. All had been willing to accept at least the symbolic power which Islam offered to the struggle against the Shah. However, the question of whether the Islamic element of the revolution should be institutionalized in the replacement state structure was an entirely different matter.

As Benard and Khalizad emphasize, the political environment shortly after the ousting of the Shah seemed more favorable to the political ascendance of modernists such as Bani-Sadr (Benard, 1984; Khalizad, 1984). The rise of Khomeini can be credited to his use of theological innuendo coupled with nationalistic fervor.[4]

Initially, the justification for Khomeini's rule was largely inferred, not only from his charismatic role as a leader of the people, but from what was "thought but not said" about Khomeini and the Twelfth Imam. In "Twelver Shi'ism", which is the predominant sect of Shi'ism in contemporary Iran, followers believe that the Twelfth Imam (chief executor and interpreter of the law) disappeared in the year 874. Many of Khomeini's followers believe that he is that "Hidden Imam", a very heretical interpretation of Shi'i doctrine, but one which Khomeini managed to sustain, while never directly endorsing (Piscatori, 1988). It was much later that Khomeini attempted to formalize his claim to power through a very liberal addition to Shi'i political doctrine. Specifically, Khomeini has legitimized his rule outright by defining himself as the "*velayat-i-faqih*" (religious jurist) and claiming that *faqihs* are the successors of the Prophet Mohammed after the Imams (Bayat, 1985). Justification for the formal statement of the political primacy of the "governance of the jurist" arose out of Khomeini's statements that the most learned in Iranian society must not lend support to secular leaders, but must lead themselves. It was they who had the true legitimate right to political leadership (Bayat, 1985).

In defining himself as the *velayat-i-faqih* and establishing the right of the Shi'i clergy to wield political power, tactical control over Iranian politics was subjected to an institutional change (Rosen, 1985). Yet, Khomeini's hold on power was clearly not the result of the success of any coherent Islamic program that he has put forward. The Islamization of the social order remained the primary task, and Khomeini used the power of Islam to change the normative order of the Iranian state (Ramazani, 1986). Indeed, Clifford Geertz's concep-tion of the state as a normative order seems particularly applicable to the Ira-nian case (Geertz, 1980).

Specifically, the language of Islam has retained its primacy during the institutionalization phase. Khomeini practiced selective adaptation and creative improvisation vis-à-vis Shi'i doctrine. There was no clear rejection of the nation state, and in fact he used Persian nationalism when useful, for example to rally the people behind the state in the war with Iraq. Attempts to frame this war as an "intra-Islamic war" must be regarded skeptically in the face of evidence that there was a much clearer connection between allegiance to the state and the threat to that state in the form of the 1980 Iraqi invasion (Ramazani, 1986).

Neither Khomeini's foreign policy nor his domestic programs pointed to the existence of a definitive plan for a new Iranian entity. As Piscatori emphasizes in his book *Islam in a World of Nation States*, the current emphasis of Islamic fundamentalists on the nation state seems to be contradictory given the traditional notion of the international 'umma. The pan-Islamic ideal of a world without nation states seems almost soley rhetorical at this juncture. This is evidenced by Khomeini's vascillation between justifying himself as a religious leader or as the savior of the Iranian nation. Furthermore, the legitimacy that the Ayatollah gained internally did not seem to depend upon his vision of a pan-Islamic community. Rather, his appeal was clearly tied to the vision of a nation forging its own path in the international arena; a path that follows "neither East nor West." (Irfani, 1983).

Therefore, if "Iranian Shi'ism" served as the vehicle for collective mobilization in the first phase of the revolution, it has been the legitimating force behind a new normative order at the state level in the second phase. Khomeini used Shi'i doctrine and shaped it in an effort to consolidate the notion of governance of the jurists. The degree of power that the state has in the Iranian context has not changed as a result of the revolution; the most dramatic change has been in regards to who is wielding that power.

Under the Shah the justification of the state was reliant upon visions of political and military power. This normative purpose has been transformed in the Islamic Republic. Political and military power are now described as tools for the moral war which the nation of Iran must wage. It is fighting the western conception of the international order, but even more than that it is fighting the western conception of morality. This we saw in the Salman Rushdie affair, in which the Ayatollah threw away the efforts of so-called "moderates" in his government to achieve reconciliation with the west, in favor of making a dramatic statement about the values of Islam.[5]

While the Shah used oppressive tactics to further the national "integration" of his nation, Khomeini used similar tactics to further the cultural integration of Iran. Alternative cultural identities such as ethnic group (the Azerbaijanis) or non-Muslim religious identification (the Baha'is, the Jews) have been rejected in the Islamic Republic. Those who are not followers of Islam, those who did not accept Khomeini's interpretation of political Shi'ism were marginalized. Khomeini promulgated a vision of the good citizen which relied upon acceptance of a new normative order. The policies of the state clearly became secondary to the moral correctness of having a legitimate ruler at the helm.

Now, in the post-Khomeini phase, political legitimacy remains with the clergy, but more emphasis is placed on the policies of the Iranian state. There seems to be no empirical basis upon which to justify the notion of a withering away of the state. The Khomeini regime pushed a new Iranian vision of the world, one which was rooted deeply in the cultural beliefs of the people. Ramazani described this phenomenon in the following passage:

> This view of the world is compatible with the Shia cultural tradition. The conflict between the camp of the oppressors and that of the oppressed resembles significantly the classical theme of conflict between right and might as enshrined in the Shia epic battle at Karbala (A.D. 681)...Khomeini's view of the world, it seems to me, also reflects the pre-Islamic Iranian cultural tradition, a tradition that insists on the incessant struggle between the forces of good and evil and the inevitable triumph of the former. (Ramazani, 1986: 24)

Conclusion

The major conclusions which I draw from this effort to reexamine the Iranian Revolution as a two-phase phenomenon, and most importantly as an essentially cultural phenomenon, are the following:

1. Laitin (1986:4) defined a cultural framework as one which considered "both faces" of culture. Firstly, the culture that lends meaning to political language in a given society and secondly, the culture that mobilizes political action in that same setting. This paper has attempted to show that Islam is best conceived of as a cultural force in the Iranian revolution, and that indeed phase one saw the mobilizational face of Shi'i Islam while phase two saw the power it has to redefine the normative order of the state through the development of a new political vocabulary.

2. It is essential that the uniqueness of Iranian Shi'ism be considered in an analysis of the role of Islam in the Revolution. It cannot rightly be conceived of as a purely religious force. Rather, as many distinguished analysts have pointed out, the connections between the Shi'ism of the Revolution and pre-Pahlavi and even pre-Islamic Iran must be taken into account. Of particular salience in this context is the psycho-historical profile of the Iranian, a person who has felt oppressed by illegitimate internal forces and zealous external forces throughout history.

3. Islam became a tool for the revolutionary movement after the initial impetus to revolt had already spread through nearly all segments of the society. It was not the raison d'être of the revolution; it was a symbolic and organizational force behind the people. However, in the second phase of the revolution, Ayatollah Khomeini's normative definition of the state and of his place in the state structure were determined by his interpretation of the political demands of Shi'ism.

NOTES

1 Piscatori (1988) drew reference to the contemporary convergence between the Shi'ite notion of fitna, which he translates as "revolt against authority", and the Sunni concept of jihad, "struggle against non-believers". Specifically, he has pointed to the common notion that a Muslim believer must now "take his fate in his own hands", and struggle outwardly for social justice.

2 This dialogue over whether the essential character of the Iranian Revolution was religious, political or economic can be seen especially in many of the writings of American academics. For example, Floor (1980): "The Revolutionary Character of the Iranian Ulama: Wishful Thinking or Reality?"; Halliday (1983): "The Iranian Revolution: Uneven Development and Religious Populism"; Keddie (1980): "Is Shi'ism Revolutionary?" The point which this paper has attempted to make is that a cultural framework can subsume all of these different aspects of the revolution under one general variable.

3 Limbert (1987); Keddie (1981); Rajaee (1989) and Behnam (1986) are just some of the analysts who have given great emphasis to this very important psychological aspect of Iranian history. Specifically, the notion is that throughout the history of modern day Iran, the people have been almost continuously subjected to cultural and/or military invasions from abroad. One interesting aspect of this is that Islam itself was imposed upon the Persians following the Arab invasion in the seventh century A.D. (Behnam, 1986).

4 By "nationalistic fervor", I refer to the way in which Khomeini was able to achieve unprecedented anti-Shah mobilization by playing upon the theme of American control over Iran. This control was thought to be political, economic and cultural.

5 February 1989 was a watershead month for the ideological crusade of the Ayatollah Khomeini. Worldwide attention was focused on Iran's leader, as he issued a death sentence, complete with ransom money for any Muslim who kill Indian author Salman Rushdie for his blasphemous novel *Satanic Verses*. This event served as an indicator that spreading and protecting the cultural power of the Islamic message still topped the Ayatollah's agenda, despite talk of "Iranian moderates" and their desire to patch up relations with western nations.

Ideology and Revolution in Iran*

FARIDEH FARHI**

ABSTRACT

The purpose of this article is to map out the role played by ideology in mass mobilization for socio-political change as well as in defending and consolidating the Iranian Revolution. To do this, a conception of ideology as a dynamic and on-going social process is forwarded. The argument is that in Iran, as in other revolutionary cases, the ideological process throught which a particular view of the world came to dominate revolutionary rhetoric was important in creating the boundaries within which the new social reality was created. This does not mean that ideological mobilization against the Shah's regime by itself can explain the outbreak, processes and outcome of the Revolution. Rather, it simply suggests that ideology is an important explanatory factor together with the political and socio-economic factors. Hence, the ideological process through which the Islamic activists became interested in gaining state power reveals much about the tenacity with which they have fended off opposition as well as the emphasis they have given to changes in the cultural sphere.

THE CONCEPTUALIZATION of the role of ideology in revolutionary processes and outcomes has been a highly contested issue. Theda Skocpol (1985: 91), I think correctly, has rejected the influence of "idea systems deployed by self-conscious political arguments by identifiable political actors". Yet, at the same time, in her attempt to combat the "purposive image" she goes too far. Although I agree with her that "innovative revolutionary propaganda retailed to the masses overnight" (Skocpol, 1982: 275-6) do not determine revolutionary processes and outcomes, a more rigorous analysis is needed to account for the exact role ideological factors play in promoting social action. In this paper, I would like to map out the role played by ideology in mass mobilization for socio-political change as well as in defending and consolidating a victorious revolution. I will begin with some of the theoretical presuppositions that underlie the writing of this paper. I will then use this analysis to explain how Islamic activism in its Iranian version was produced and transformed historically. The role of ideological factors in restructuring the Iranian post-revolutionary society will be discussed in the last part of the paper.

* A different version of this paper was presented at the conference on ''The Iranian Revolution in Comparative Perspective'', held by the Center for Middle Eastern Studies, Harvard University on 18-19 January, 1989. I would like to thank Quee-Young Kim for helpful suggestions.
** Department of Political Science, University of Hawaii at Manoa, Honolulu, HI 96813, U.S.A.

Theoretical Considerations

The most important presupposition in this paper is the rejection of ideology as a mere system of ideas. Rather, ideology is conceived as a dynamic, ongoing *social process* through which subjects are created and yet, at the same time, is subject to transformation by the willful actions of more or less knowledgeable actors. As such, following Therborn (1980, 2), ideology is "that aspect of human condition under which human being live their lives as conscious actors in a world that makes sense to them to varying degrees". Hence, it must be understood by aligning it, not with self-consciously held political beliefs, but with the large cultural systems that preceded it, and out of which, as well as against which, it came into being. This does not mean that there are no distinctions between culture and ideology. Clearly, real cultures entail diverse, often conflicting symbols, stories, rituals and world-views from which actors select different strategies for action (Swidler, 1986). Ideologies, on the other hand, are highly articulated cultural models aspiring to offer one unified answer to the question of how human beings should live and act. As such they are produced to alter the existing world-views and assumptions. Yet, even during ideologically charged periods, as Swidler points out (1986: 279) they are deeply connected to the cultures in which they are embedded. This is because:

> [r]ather than providing the underlying assumptions of an entire way of life, they make explicit demands in a contested cultural arena. Their independent cultural influence is limited...because, at least at their origins, such ideological movements are not complete culture, in the sense that much of their taken-for-granted understanding of the world and many of their daily practices still depend on traditional patterns.

Of course, over time, ideology may deepen its critique of the existing order and begin to unsettle even the taken-for-granted areas of everyday life. But important linkages to the old cultural order remain that need to be investigated in order to shed light on the available strategies of action. After all, if we accept culture as a "tool-kit" of diverse strategies for action, then the existing cultural order qualifies people to "take up and perform the repertoire of roles given in the society into which they are born, including the role of possible agents of social change" (Therborn, 1980, 17).[1] And, it is during these periods of rapid social change that cultural meanings wear the mask of ideology as they become highly articulated and explicit in order to forward patterns of action that are easily perceived. This process which Therborn (1980, 120-1) calls ideological mobilization involves:

> setting a common agenda for a mass of people—that is to say, summing up the dominant aspect or aspects of the crisis, identifying the crucial target, the essence of evil, and defining what is possible and how it should be achieved. Such mobilization develops through a breach in the regime's matrix of affirmations and sanctions, which in normal times ensures compromise or acquiescence and the successful sanctioning of oppositional forces. This breach grows to the extent that it is itself successfully affirmed in the practice of demonstrations, acts of insubordination and revolt, and so on. A successful ideological mobilization is alway translated or manifested in practices of political mobilization.

This does not mean that the process of ideological mobilization is self-consistent. Indeed, it is generally imbued with the contradictory and antagonistic action of a large number of actors or groups of actors. But successful ideological mobilization always manages to fuse and condense several ideological discourses into a single major theme, usually expressed in a single slogan. For our purposes, the interesting question relates to the process through which certain groups become the "real" articulators of this major theme. Hence, we need not only to understand how, given the existing cultural models, a particular highly organized meaning system gains currency but also understand why one ideology rather than another triumphs. This is a task that can only be accomplished through the historical analysis of particular cases. But, concrete historical forms of ideological mobilization have given us clues about several sources the revolutionaries can draw upon in order to mobilize.

The most important source seems to be the "dangerous" memory of conflict and exclusion (Welsh, 1985, ch. 3). This memory has two dimensions, that of suffering and that of resistance and hope. The former draws from concrete memories of oppression and suffering. "It declares that such suffering matters; the oppression of the people is of ultimate concern" (Ibid.: 36). Hence past suffering becomes an indictment of existing economic and political systems. Memory of resistance and hope, on the other hand, chronicles actual, or imagined, instances of resistance and liberation. These accounts are a declaration of the possibility of change, and they are examined continuously in an attempt to understand what enables resistance in specific, historical situations. They are also generally reenacted in symbolic fashion through plays, sermons, religious ceremonies, etc. in order to sustain the revolutionary fervor. The ultimate result is the creation and sustenance of "[t]he memory of a community in which people were free to claim an identity different from that imposed on them. It is both a memory of past liberation and a motivation for further liberation. It is a memory of resistance and of hope for further resistance" (Ibid. 42).

It is important to point out that the "true" retrieval and propagation of an actual event is not at issue here. Rather, it is the process of *imagining* and *creation* of the memory, and the struggles associated with this process, that matters. To be sure, the particular memory of suffering and resistance may be connected to an actual event but it is the manner in which that event is constructed that ultimately becomes a source for mobilization. This is why the historical context of the event itself (at least in terms of time and geography) is not relevant in the creation of the memory. The memory of resistance, as in the case of Iran, may draw from a timeless past; a past that reportedly witnessed the martyrdom of a religious leader in his attempt to institute the true, just Islamic society. Or, as in the case of Nicaragua, the memory may go beyond the geographical and national boundaries and draw from the experiences of other people perceived to be in a similar situation (i.e., Cuba). In all cases, the memory itself is dynamic in so far as it changes with the deepening of the revolutionary crisis.

But why do certain memories of exclusion and conflict begin to gain hold during the revolutionary process? The central argument of this paper is that the imagination and creation of "dangerous" memory must be understood as it emerges from the ruins of the pre-revolutionary ideological structures. This is because ideological mobilization always entails two processes: the decomposition of the old and the recomposition of the new one. These are interrelated processes as the contested existing orders are quite resilient and leave their mark defining certain possibilities and impossibilities for the emerging meaning system. Hence a close look at the ideological glue that held the old regime together is important not only in order to understand the contradictions that unravelled the ideological hold of the old regime but also in order to lay out the recomposition of the new one. This is a theoretical contention that will now be demonstrated by sketching an account of ideological change in the Iranian Revolution.

The Ideology of the Prerevolutionary Regime

The ideological foundation of the Iranian prerevolutionary regime was complex and contradictory. As in most peripheral formations, the complexities and contradictions were related to the disjunctions between the structure and behavior of the prerevolutionary state and the two important ideological discourses that accompanied its modern state formation: modernization (economic as well as political) and nationalism. The undemocratic (and in many ways archaic) structure of the Iranian state and its emergence through the defeat of nationalist forces clearly contrasted with the image the Iranian leadership felt obligated to portray. Accordingly, the Shah's regime developed fairly complex sets of arguments and symbols to account for and to camouflage this disparity. Ultimately, however, as with the other social structures, these ideological webs failed, allowing other ideological forces to mobilize.

More specifically, the ideological foundation of the Iranian regime had two components: official nationalism[2] and the defense of the monarchy as the true representative of progressive/modernizing/democratizing forces. The official nationalism of Mohammad Reza Pahlavi developed after the defeat of the oil nationalization movement in the 1950s. In order to gain legitimacy, the Shah's regime coopted much of the language and issues used by the nationalist movements. Hence, control over oil production and profits became an ideological cornerstone of the new regime. The Shah not only did not denationalize the oil industry, he portrayed himself as the champion of the Iranian cause. This was despite the fact that Iranian oil production and exports effectively remained in the hands of foreigners until the 1970s (Halliday, 1979: 140-6). Once fundamental changes did occur in the patterns of control through the coordinated pressure of the Organization of Petroleum Exporting Countries (OPEC), much was made of the Shah's leadership role in bringing about that change.

Much was also made of Iran embarking on the path of industrialization.

In fact, the language of progress slowly began to replace the nationalist discourse. If indeed Iran was going to "catch up with the West soon", then there was no contradiction between Iranian national aspirations and the close relationship developed with the West in general and America in particular. It was not foreign control that held Iran back, official rhetoric implied, but lack of proper technology, skills, attitudes and ideas—all of which could be bought or emulated from the West. And Iran, unlike many other peripheral formations, could overcome the hurdle of backwardness because of access to oil revenues and her long and distinguished past. I have already mentioned how oil had become connected to nationalism. The reference to Iranian history, however, requires more elaboration since it relates to the anti-Islamic bent of the regime.

Modern Iranian political thought had been preoccupied with the issue of nationalism since the end of the nineteenth century. While any summary does injustice to the complexity of debates within modern Iranian political theory, it is fair to say that the relationship of Iranian nationalism to Islam was the most contentious part of the debate. Some theorists called for unity around Islam to fend off the West. Others, on the other hand, rejected Islam by interpreting Iranian history as one of defeat, passivity and corruption after Islam and the "inferior" Arabs "conquered" Iran. These writers looked to the great pre-Islamic Persian Empires for nationalist inspiration. As Keddie (1981: 183-202) points out, both Islamic and anti-Islamic nationalisms were multiclass phenomena but it was the latter that was picked up by the Pahlavi dynasty. Keddie (Ibid.: 191-2) also suggests an explanation of why this interpretation of the Iranian past, at least for a while, was not contested:

> The Pahlavi Shahs picked up pre-Islamic Iranian nationalism, cut off the radical elements that were central to its chief intellectual advocates (especially the communist religion and revolt of the fifth century A.D. heretic Mazdak), and made it a foundation of anticlerical monarchism. This use of it was probably no more forced than the other, as the two great pre-Islamic empires were strong monarchies; on the other hand popular elements could be found in pre-Islamic religions such as Mazdakism, Manichaeism and Zoroastrianism, as could evidence that women and agriculturalists enjoyed higher respect in some pre-Islamic periods that in the nineteenth century. The main appeal of an idealized distant past, however, whether Islamic or pre-Islamic, was and is that a great variety of values may be read into it, while the evils of the present can be ascribed to deviation from the true Iranian and true Islamic essence. In a period when all society was at least formally Islamic, it was natural for many thinkers to blame Iran's problems on Islam and the Arabs, and to see in a nationalist interpretation of the distant Iranian past virtues that were often modern or Western ones.

This use of Iranian pre-Islamic history also lent itself to the defense of monarchy as a proper method of rule. The Pahlavi dynasty, since it had usurped power relatively recently, did not benefit from the blood lineage that usually gives legitimacy to hereditary rule. Instead, it tried to represent itself as the "true" heir of the "glorious" Persian tradition. Hence, the task of the monarchy was portrayed as one of reestablishing Iranian greatness in the international arena. No longer was the monarchy to be perceived as an archaic institution. Rather, its mission was to modernize Iran. If its monarchical form did not seem particularly modern, it had less to do with the desires and actions of the monarch—who was presumably a democrat at heart—and more to do with the exigencies of backwardness in Iran. After all, what could be more progressive and democratic than redistribution of land to the peasants, extension of suffrage to women, and creation of a national literacy corps, all instituted by royal decree during the White Revolution (later renamed The Shah-People Revolution) in the 1960s. These policies were complemented with the almost daily repetition and celebration of the monarch's role in "civilizing" Iran. The attempt was to create an almost god-like image for him.[3] God-like because it constituted the monarch as the creator of modern Iran as well as a body to be feared. Ironically, in many ways, it was the success of this ideological construction that ultimately proved problematic. The Shah was accepted as the creator but he was also seen as responsible for the results. He was feared but he was also loathed. In other words, it was the thinnes of the lines that separate creation from responsibility and fear from hatred that opened the way to the possibility of ideological opposition in Iran.

Of course, the Shah's regime was not thrown into crisis because of its ideological make-up. As suggested elsewhere (Farhi, 1988), the revolution was launched by a crisis centered around the structure and situation of the Pahlavi state within the domestic and international fields surrounding it. But once the crisis had begun, the ideological make-up of the regime contributed to the direction of the revolutionary process. As it will be shown in the next section, the clerical aspiration to gain state power reflected important changes within the Islamic community. But the appeal of this Islamic vision to all sectors of the Iranian society, for at least a historical moment, was made possible by the ideological make-up of the old regime.

The Ascent of Islamic Activism

In several scholarly works it has been noted that Shi'ism has especially salient features that pose potential threat to the state authority (Algar, 1969; Keddie, 1972)). The Shi'ite Doctrine of Imamate, for instance, ascribes legitimate rule to the Imams who were descendants of Ali, the successor of the Prophet and the first Shi'ite Imam. Since the Occultation of the last Imam in the ninth century, however, legitimate authority in the Shi'ite community has fallen into the hands of the Ulama who, as representatives of the will of the Imam, claimed the right to guide the community of believers.[4] Since the Shi'ites presumably do not differentiate between political and religious spheres, a tension has always existed between religious authority and political power. Stories abound about the struggles staged by various Imams in the just cause of resisting usurping temporal rulers (Fischer, 1980: 12-27). One such story is especially heartrending. It involves the third Imam, Hosain, who bravely faced martyrdom in his attempt to institute the true and just Islamic society. This incident is used in religious preachments, and especially during the month of Muharran when the incident is celebrated, to place responsibility in the Shi'ite community for not helping the Imam institute the just Islamic society.

Despite the tension existing between religious authority and political power in theory, the Ulama have generally cooperated with the rulers and legitimized their power throughout the course of Iranian history. That is, in practice, they have accepted the existence of temporal power and limited their leadership to the religious sphere. The political and anti-imperialist role of the clergy that emerged at the end of the Qajar period, therefore, has not been treated, by most scholars, as a political development logically deduced from Shi'ite doctrines. Rather, the rift between the Ulama and the Qajar state has been regarded as a nationalist response to Western influence and the increasing incorporation of Iran into the Western political and economic structures (Algar, 1969; Keddie, 1966). Later, the rift was also based on the threats posed to the religious leadership by a secular state which used military-bureaucratic reorganization to institute administrative, legal, economic and educational reforms based on Western ideas—all of which were intended to enhance the power of the state vis-à-vis groups in the civil society.

The development of an activist posture by the Ulama did not mean a unified and/or consistent oppositional stance towards the state even when the religious establishment was severely attacked by the state (e.g., during Reza Shah's reign). Two aspects of state/Ulama relationship can help explain this. First, the lack of a single, unified and disciplined hierarchy, and the ties that developed between some leading members of the religious establishment and the state which created schisms within the religious community with respect to the institution of monarchy. For instance, in his detailed analysis of state/Ulama relations, Akhavi (1980) reports on the various positions—ranging from active support to rejection—taken by the leading clergy during the nationalist period in the 1950s and the 1963 uprising. Second, when the Ulama's prerogatives have been effectively and suddenly attacked, as they were under Reza Shah, the religious community has found it difficult to gather resources and prepare to counterattack.

This brief elaboration on the history of the Ulama/state relationship immediately brings forth an important question: What were the added factors that propelled the Ulama not only to oppose the monarchy but also to aspire to control the state? Three factors seem particularly important: 1) reemergence of Islamic nationalism; 2) development of an ideological basis for the control of the state; and 3) the organizational prowess of the clergy. In the following pages I will lay out these factors and will argue that some of them had been present throughout the twentieth century but became intensified during the prerevolutionary period while others were new and related to the particular form into which the state/Ulama relationship was molded during Mohammad Reza Shah's reign.

Re-emergence of Islamic nationalism. As mentioned earlier, the development

of Shi'ism into a form of nationalism expressed in terms of the dominant
cultural form went back to the advent of Western penetration. As Bashiriyeh
(1984: 53-4) explains:

> The increasing competition of foreign interests undermined the traditional petty com-
> modity production centered in the bazaars. As a result the traditional petty bourgeoisie
> emerged as the social basis of resistance to western economic, political and cultural influ-
> ence as the stronghold of nationalism... It was from this conjuncture of interactions
> between Iranian and Western economies that early Iranian nationalism emerged as a pro-
> test movement. It was also the nature of this conjuncture that gave Iranian nationalism
> its particular characteristics: nationalism was expressed in terms of Islam and Islam was
> expressed in terms of nationalism.

In the more recent period, this form of nationalism once again reappeared
as the economic and socio-political position of the petty bourgeoisie of the
bazaar, which had historically been the social basis of indigenous Islamic
nationalism, began to deteriorate. The most persistent articulator of this
rejuvenated nationalism was, of course, Ayatollah Khomeini who, from exile,
preached against "the ever increasing blows against Islam, the enserfment of
the nation by the imperialists and their control of the bazaars and all military,
political and commercial aspects of life" (quoted in Ibid.: 61).

Khomeini was undoubtedly the hero of the bazaar petty bourgeoisie. But,
this rejuvenated Islamic nationalism was much more broad-based.[5] By the
1970s, it also attracted the young intelligentsia who had become concerned
about Western cultural domination. This was an important development
because this social grouping had traditionally shown affinities with secular
opposition. However, the need to differentiate from anything Westernized
made these ideologies—also identified with the West—less appealing. Furthermore, as mentioned above, since "nationalism with a pre-Islamic emphasis
had been largely coopted by the Shah, the only competing ideology with the
hope of mass support was some version of Shi'i Islam" (Keddie, 1982: 290).[6]
With the deepening of the revolutionary crisis, even the professional middle
class, a class which was by and large the product of the Shah's state and was
fairly inculcated with western values, relented and accepted the Islamic leadership. By this time, as Arjomand (1988: 109) reports, Khomeini was seen as the
embodiment of Iranian tradition, totally uncontaminated by the cultural
alienation wrought be western penetration.

The popularity of the works of the popular lay ideologist, Ali Shariati, is
just one example of the yearning for a "pure" national identity. Although
partly anti-clerical, Shariati sought to restore the political role of religion and
lay the theoretical foundation for a new Islamic political community. This new
Islamic political community was derived from the active rejection of the West
and an emphasis on the local economy and culture. Through the advocacy of
"active" rejection, Shariati was attempting to do away with the traditional
notion that one must passively wait for the end of the era of occultation until
a just, Islamic government could be established. Because of this, he became
very popular among the urban educated youth, predominantly from *bazaari*

background. He was especially appreciated by radical Islamic organizations such as the Mojahedin-e Khalq whose political agenda was based on a radical interpretation of Islam with a very strong anti-capitalist and anti-imperialist bent.

Development of the ideological basis for control of the state. On a more fundamental level, the essence of Shariati's thought hinted at the development of a new approach to the question of political authority. The schism between political and religious authorities that had characterized the Iranian community was no longer deemed satisfactory. The combination of this and the activist posture he advocated clearly called for an attack on the state and its reshaping according to Islamic principles. Shariati, however, was not very clear about how the Islamic ethos (as interpreted by him) of his imagined community was going to reshape social, political and legal institutions (Akhavi, 1983). A much more coherent approach to the post-revolutionary state was developed by Khomeini who coined the saying that Ulama should rule directly on behalf of the Hidden Imam.

The idea that Ulama should rule directly and its accompanying corollary that monarchy was illegitimate in Islam, was indeed a very radical idea within Shi'ism. It negated both the quietism of the first centuries after the Occultation and the parliamentary constitutional view that was predominant among the clerical reformers. As Floor (1980) has indicated, in the twentieth century most Ulama, particularly the higher ones, have been more conservative than revolutionary in their opposition, they wished to stop Western penetration and influence, not to create a new system of rule and society. The cardinal question, therefore, is related to circumstances that led to the ascent of this radical position within the religious community.

Unfortunately, while many scholars have been quick to point out the emergence of this radical position, they have not been as successful in forwarding an adequate explanation for this change. The answers that emphasize the intensity of socio-economic transformations can explain protests against the regime but cannot explain the noted change in the nature of these protests. The only satisfactory answer, to my mind, has been put forth by Enayat (1983) who argues that the answer must be found in the processes and outcomes of the state-Ulama struggles from the end of the nineteenth century. He specifically points to four episodes that have been instrumental in bringing about a political transformation within Shi'ism: the "Tobacco Rebellion" of 1892, the Constitutional Revolution of 1906-11, the oil nationalization movement of 1951-3, and the abortive uprising of 1963 led by Khomeini. With regard to processes, these episodes were similar, he argues, in that they all required an alliance among the main social and political forces in the country (the Ulama, the indigenous propertied class and secular nationalists), and they were all dependent on active encouragement of the religious leaders to mobilize the masses.

With the exception of the 1963 uprising,[7] these events were also similar with regard to outcomes:

[O]n each occasion, while the religious leaders emerged as *immediate* beneficiaries, on each occasion too, either the government or the semi-secular nationalists soon managed to gain the upper hand, and excluded their religious partners from power... Accordingly, the Ulama genuinely drew three lessons from these: (i) whenever they campaign, there is nothing which can stand in their way of immediate success; (ii) in order to ensure the consummation of their success, they should not trust or share power with their secular or semi-secular rivals; (iii) the defeat of 1963 showed that religious leadership cannot have any hope of initial success unless it manages to have a degree of internal unity (Ibid.: 198-9). (emphasis in original)

The previous political experience, therefore, set the stage for a reevaluation of the goals of the religious movement and opened the way for the ascent of the radical position. The mastery of popular movement was no longer deemed sufficient; the new resolve was to prevent others from usurping the fruits of religious efforts, namely state power.[8]

Organizational prowess. If the ideological maturation made the militant wing of the religious movement determined not to allow itself to be outwitted by the assortment of secular forces, it was their organizational capabilities that made popular mobilization and continued mastery over the popular movement possible. The Iranian religious community has always had certain economic, political and cultural resources that have given the Ulama the organizational independence to react against state encroachments. The most important political resource was located in the fact that the Ulama's leadership resided in the Shi'i shrine cities in Iraq, uncontrolled by Iran's government. Economic resources have included the control over charitable/religious endownments (*vaqf*) given for institutions such as schools, mosques, shrines and hospitals. The Ulama have also kept direct control over certain religious taxes, the so-called *khoms* (one-fifth) and *zakat* (alms) and the voluntary *sadaqat* and *nuzur* (vows). According to Keddie (1981: 17), it is known that "the Ulama were able to use a combination of moral and physical pressure to collect, especially from the merchants and other well-off bazaar traders and artisans, the khums". Furthermore, Keddie goes on to say, while most if this was supposed to go to welfare and charity, a large sum contributed to a significant net increase in the wealth and power of the religious classes.[9] These advantages were complemented by long-established networks of associations, mostly created to promote religious observance and to celebrate Shi'i festivals. Like the Christian-based communities in Nicaragua, these associations ultimately proved indispensable in organizing the urban poor during the revolutionary crisis.

All these resources available to the Shi'i formed a significant basis for Ulama's activism. However, it is important not to carry this point too far. An independent financial basis did not always lead to financial security and/or independent political activities. As Algar (1969: 16) reports on the conditions during the Qajar Dynasty, the control of much of *vaqf* property was in the hands of the state, and "the yearly grants made to the Ulama...could on occasion be intended as silence money". In addition, dependence on individual contributions tended to make the Ulama subservient to pressures of public opinion. It was the existence of these weaknesses that allowed Reza Shah to attack religious institutions as ferociously as possible without instigating massive resistance.

After Reza Shah's abdication, however, there was a gradual rebuilding of clerical power and organization that can help explain clerical success in 1979. It is important to lay out these changes since they took place in a round-about way despite continued governmental attacks against some clerical prerogatives. The first change entailed the evolution of an efficient system, centered in the city of Qom, for the collection and distribution of religious taxes and alms.[10] This system was developed by Ayatollah Borujerdi, the sole "source of imitation" between 1947 and 1961, at a time when political quietism was encouraged by the religious leadership. But it created a sounder financial basis for the religious community and a network of communication directly linked to Qum that were later used by Islamic militants to foster more activist orientation.

The second change entailed the emergence of a new religious stratum. As mentioned, in the past the Ulama were largely dependent for their financial resources on the populace, although some were under the state's direct pay. The expansion of the state and the availability of more varied resources, however, gave rise to a new stratum which was relatively independent from both public donations and direct state support. Enayat (1983: 203-4) explains this phenomenon and its consequences for the religious community:

> Thanks to a variety of fresh job opportunities—teaching in non-religious institutions, schools and universities, journalism, publishing, etc.—they were able to earn enough to be independent of both the patriarchal Ulama and the state if they wanted to— although in terms of religious dogma they were inevitably affiliated to one or the other of the Ulama. This brought them nearer to other groups of educated people—teachers, lectures, writers and intellectuals in general—with all that is meant in terms of exposure to radicalizing currents, and response to social and political strains. Much of, but by no means all, the ideological and organizational work which consciously or unconsciously prepared the ground for the religious leadership of the Revolution, especially the political use of the mosques, was done by this group.

It was this group that created the necessary ideological bridge between the religious community and the rest of the society. But, more importantly, it was this group that, by incorporating ideas developed by theorists like Shariati, pushed the religious community as a whole towards militancy. And, it was this militancy that allowed the transformation of the already existing networks of religious associations into political ones. These associations gave the religious community an organizational resource not available to others and, hence, facilitated the making of religion into the dominant form of political expression (Kazemi, 1980: 94).

Islamic Activism and Revolutionary Outcome

To discuss the outcome of recent revolutions is a chancy exercise. Much of the problem lies with the term "outcome", which connotes an observable and fixed result, at the time when the revolutionary process is still unfolding. The historical proximity of the Iranian Revolution clearly does not afford the long-term hindsight needed to unravel its general character. Yet, there are certain important features that are observable even now. For instance, the revolutionary regime has consolidated power effectively and has overseen the development of a more bureaucratized state capable of maintaining the support of relatively large sectors of the population (Arjomand, 1988; Bakhash, 1984). In addition, the regime has been able to carry out some of its programs despite the burden of a major war that has caused hundreds of thousands of casualties and has resulted in billions of dollars of property damage. But the success of the Islamic revolutionaries, so far, has been mostly limited to the political and cultural arenas. As is well-known, a theocratic and stable state intent on remolding people's "ways of life" has been instituted. And, the results of this generalized commitment to Islamic principles have been unambiguous. The monarchy has been abolished and the elite directly associated with it have been displaced. The administrative, judicial and coercive apparatuses, have been reorganized and used for vicious attacks on the lifestyles and institutional supports of social groupings with supposed links to the West as well as those opposed to the regime for any reason. Yet, this brutal and successful neutralization or elimination of all opposition groups has been done without the destruction of the repressive apparatus connected to the old regime. To be sure, desired changes to assure the control of state apparatus have been made but these changes have been mostly limited to decapitation as the prerevolutionary leaders were replaced by loyalists. Even the old imperial army has been maintained and, in fact, after the early weakening due to the liquidation of its leadership, it has been slowly rehabilitated by the war with Iraq.

Even less change has occurred in the economic sphere. So far, the Islamic revolutionaries have not been able to devise, much less institute, an "Islamic" economic plan that would clearly differentiate them from their predecessors. In other words, no systematic effort to articulate, let alone implement, a comprehensive program of economic and social reforms has been made. No land reform has been agreed upon, agricultural production is under-utilized, unemployment is rampant and not even a literacy campaign has been promulgated. In general, although the banking system and some industries have been nationalized, there has not been much change in the structure of the economy and its continuing dependence on the export of petroleum.

What explains the peculiar outcome of the Iranian Revolution? Clearly the ideological pronouncements of the Iraniam regime are not enough. Although they use different symbolism and ideological referents, the Islamic revolutionaries have articulated goals and desires similar to the ones advocated by their counterparts in other Third World countries. In the economic sphere, they call for types of production and distribution that are oriented toward meeting the basic needs of the majority of the population. In the political sphere, they call for the reconstitution of state-society relations such that the so-called "downtrodden" classes have a higher degree of participation in determining public policy. And, finally, discussions of economic distribution and political participation are situated within the context of struggle against American imperialism at all levels (from economic to cultural). Yet, the Islamic revolutionaries clearly have different practices, especially in the political and economic arenas. As the recent theorists of revolutions (Skocpol, 1979; Goldstone, 1986) have reminded us, the struggle to control and maintain state power, and the preexisting political and socio-economic structures go a long way in explaining this divergence of ideology from practice.

But, this does not mean that the historical development of Islamic activism first as an oppositional ideology and then as a state ideology is of no explanatory value. As I suggested above, the pattern of ideological mobilization is always important for understanding the nature of revolutionary confrontation. Furthermore, with the victory of oppositional forces, and with its full-fledged articulation, revolutionary rhetoric takes on added importance as it sets the boundaries within which the revolutionaries operate. In the case of Iran, at least two important effects of the pattern of mobilization must be noted.

First, there is the important role played by the development of the ideological basis for the control of state power. As mentioned above, this facet of Islamic activism represented years of reflection on the history of religious opposition and its relationship to other societal forces. It was an impetus for the religious forces to seek the leadership of the oppositional movement. It also explains the tenacity with which they have clung to state power. It is true, as Skocpol (1979) suggests, that the revolutionaries' ideological vision is continuously undercut by the exigencies of the attempt to take and hold state power. But not all revolutionaries develop the determination to hold onto state power at all cost. The Iranian clerics did and this ideological basis has made it possible for them to fuse state control and religious leadership and treat the opposition to either with extreme harshness and with few qualms.

The second important role played by ideology has to do with the actual policies promulgated by the revolutionary regime. Although there has been much conflict over economic policies (e.g., land reform), there has hardly been any disagreement on the need for maintaining Islamic norms of social and gender relations, education and law. This unity of the clergy over these issues has led many observers to call the Iranian events above all a cultural revolution. But the main reason for the success of the regime in these areas has been unity of opinion. As I attempted to show above, the possibility for this unity became actualized because of a pattern of ideological mobilization which constituted the Shah and his cohorts as the source of Western values and envisioned the opposition's task as one of reinstating Islamic codes. Clearly the same process did not create a space for unity on economic and political grounds.

Conclusion

The discussion of revolutionary ideology in this paper was intended to shed light on the process through which certain ideas or slogans came to represent the struggle against the old regime in Iran. This does not mean that other ideas or slogans did not exist. Rather my point was that the process through which a particular view of the world comes to dominate revolutionary rhetoric is important for understanding the boundaries within which the "new" social reality is created. Revolutions are not purely destructive events. They are also creative in so far as they allow individuals and groups to articulate and pursue different visions of the past and the future. In this paper, I have argued that the success, at least for a historical moment, of a particular vision was dependent on the ideological structure of the old regime as well as political and organizational mutations that occurred within the opposition forces. Hence, in Iran, the official anti-Islamic nationalism of the Shah's regime made suspect other Western-derived forms of expression while organizational and political changes within the Islamic community opened the way for the ascent of radical forces. This does not mean that ideological mobilization against the Iranian regime by itself can explain the outbreak and processes of the revolution. Rather, it simply means that it is an important explanatory factor together with the political and socioeconomic factors. Similarly, ideology cannot explain revolutionary outcome by itself. But, the boundaries within which revolutionary rhetoric emerges during the revolutionary process, like the other existing structures also powerfully shapes revolutionary outcome. Hence, in Iran, the ideological process through which the Islamic activists became interested in gaining state power reveals much about the tenacity with which the Islamic revolutionaries have fended off opposition against their control of state power as well as the emphasis they have given to changes in the cultural sphere.

NOTES

1   This culture-connected view of ideology differs from both the traditional Marxist approach which sees ideology as forms of consciousness either corresponding to class interest ('true' consciousness) or not ('false' consciousness). It is also different from the liberal conception (followed by Skocpol) which sees it as bodies of thought that we possess and invest in our actions. It is closer to Clifford Geertz (1973) view which sees ideologies not as distinctive kinds of belief systems but rather as distinctive phases in the development of cultural systems. On this see Swidler (1986).

2   My use of this term is influenced by Benedict Anderson's brilliant study of nationalism, *Imagined Community* (1983). Anderson borrows the term from Seton-Watson and applies it mainly to European nationalism after the 1820s.

3   One of his most commonly used life-sized portraits showed him emerging from the clouds and extending his hand toward the on-lookers, who were presumably the people in the Shah-people equation.

4   Obviously, this is a very sketchy elaboration of a very complex set of ideas. For instance, the role of Ulama is complicated by the fact that only years of religious study give some of the clerics the possibility of interpreting Imam's will. But, unlike the Imam, they remain

fallible. The purpose here, however, is to forward a general sense for the Shi'ite world view. The Revolution in Iran has brought forth a large number of excellent works on religion in Iran. See, for instance, Akhavi (1980); Arjomand (1984); and Fischer (1980).

5 As Keddie (1982: 290) points out, this is indeed the paradox of the Iranian situation: Islam came to play an even greater role in the Iranian oppositional movement, "even though the number and power of Westernized secularized Iranians had grown greatly".

6 This is not to suggest that Western-originated idea systems like Marxism were not present but simply to explain the popular appeal of Shi'i Islam as a representation of the "true" Iranian identity.

7 The 1963 uprising, which ended in a crushing defeat of the Ulama, was characterized by a rift within the religious community. The intransigent, anti-royalist stand of Khomeini created a gulf between him and the more conservative Ulama.

8 The following quote, cited by Enayat (1983: 199), from the leading Islamic thinker Morteza Motahhari, is perhaps the best indication of this sentiment: "The history of Islamic movements during the last hundred years reveals one unfortunate defect in its leadership: it has continued the struggle under its leadership [only] up to the moment of victory, but has refused to carry it on further [preferring instead] to go after its own business and allow others to usurp the results of its efforts (Ibid., p. 199).

9 These collections were used to support poor religious students who formed the immediate constituency of each of the Ulama (sometimes acting as their private armies), and employees of religious welfare institutions.

10 According to Algar (1972: 243), bookkeeping was introduced to account for the receipt and dispersion of donations, and "a register" was established of local agents authorized to collect money and forward it to Qum.

From Military to Social Revolution: A Comparative Analysis of Ethiopia and the Sudan

QUEE-YOUNG KIM AND JENNIFER M. LEACH*

ABSTRACT

This study was undertaken to establish why different revolutionary outcomes were reached in Ethiopia and the Sudan given many initial similarities between the two countries. To answer this proposed question we discuss the similarities, the differences and contrast the situation in the state structures of these countries. We find that the difference in outcomes can be explained largely in terms of the nature of the old regime, the extent of social mobilization during the revolutionary process, the strength of the military and the degree of autonomy of the revolutionary elites from the class and ethnic structure.

IN SPRING 1974, over issues of pay and morale, Ethiopian soldiers mutinied in several provinces and the taxi drivers of Addis Ababa protested a fifty percent rise in the price of petrol following the OPEC (Organization of Petroleum Exporting Countries) price increases. Students, teachers and workers joined the rising tide of protests against government corruption and demanded reforms. The government changed cabinet ministers and made some concessions only to provoke more strikes and protests. In June, the junior officers in Addis Ababa revolted and formed the Coordinating Committee of the Armed Forces, the Police and the Territorial Army: the Derg (Amharic for Committee). From June to September, the Derg orchestrated a kind of 'creeping *coup d'état*', deposed Haile Selassie, abolished the ancient monarchy and announced the Provisional Military Adminstration Council (PMAC). By 1978, Lt. Colonel Mengistu emerged as the leader of the PMAC with his autocratic, radical program. A Socialist Republic was proclaimed in 1984. The PMAC purged its enemies through terror in 1977 and 1978 and held off all threats to its power including an abortive *coup d'état* in May, 1989.

In the neighboring Sudan, on April 6, 1985 senior military officers with the support of some professional groups in Khartoum overthrew the 16-year government of President Jaafar Nimeiri. The military leaders set up a 15-member Transitional Military Council (TMC) chaired by Lt. General Abdel Rahman Suwar el-Dahab. The following year general elections were held in

* Department of Sociology, University of Wyoming, Laramie, Wyoming 82031, U.S.A.

which the Umma Party and Democratic Unionist Party gained a majority (165 out of a total of 301) of seats in the Assembly. The TMC handed over power to a civilian government headed by the Umma Party's Sadiq al-Mahdi.

The fall of Nimeiri was the fourth change of government in the Sudan's short history of independence. Since gaining its independence in 1956 from the colonialist rule of Great Britain and Egypt, the Sudan experienced three military *coups d'état*, one change of government through election, two unsuccessful coups, and an on-going civil war between the dominant, primarily Muslim, Arab-speaking north and the more rural, tribal, non-Muslim and non-Arab south. These changes of government have also been changes in style of government, with a relatively weak system of parliamentary government alternating with periods of military dictatorship. More than 60 political parties compete for power and the parliament reshuffles ministers and laws so routinely that planning has become impossible. In April 1989, the last coalition cabinet fell after just six weeks. On June 30, Lt. Gen. Omar Hassan al-Bashir staged a coup and ousted Sadiq al-Mahdi. (Our discussion is limited to the conditions of the pre-1989 coup in the Sudan because little is known about the new situation as of this writing).

Unlike most post-1945 social revolutions in the Third World, the revolutionary movements in Ethiopia and the Sudan were not made in the countryside, let alone by peasants, although land issues and peasant discontents contributed to the weakening of the regimes. They were primarily military revolutions precipiated by fiscal crises and urban protests. The purposes were not just to replace one leadership with another but to create social revolutions from above.

On the basis of her study of Japan, Turkey, Egypt and Peru, Ellen Kay Trimberger (1978: 3) proposed five criteria for revolution from above:

1. The revolution is organized and led by high military and sometimes high civilian bureaucrats of the old regime;

2. There is little or no mass participation in the military takeover or in the initiation of change;

3. The takeover and change are accompanied by little violence or resistance;

4. The change is undertaken in a pragmatic step by step manner, with little appeal to radical ideology; and

5. Military bureaucrats who lead a revolution from above destroy the economic and political base of the aristocracy or upper class.

The experiences of Ethiopia and the Sudan under Mengistu and Nimeiri contradict some of these operational features such as lack of terror and pragmatic approach. The overthrow of Emperor Haile Selassie in 1974 had some urban but no nationwide mass participation. Ethiopian military elites resorted to radical ideology. Nimeiri was overthrown by high level military bureaucrats, there was no significant mass participation in the action taken, the takeover was achieved with little violence, but change was made in a haphazard way, resorting later to radical Islamization, and the economic and political base of the upper class was not destroyed.

Trimberger's criteria are not useful in leading us to the distinctions between the military and social revolution or in generating explanations based on a distinction between the actions of the military regime and its outcomes. The overthrow of Emperor Haile Selassie in 1974 was only the beginning of a widespread revolution that resulted in the near-total destruction of the feudal class and landed aristocracy. Additionally, the institution of a new socialist-oriented government occurred. All of this was achieved by the military with the support, at least initially, of a broad, cross-class coalition of Ethiopians. The military revolution in Ethiopia, in short, created "a rapid, fundamental, and violent domestic change in the dominant values and myths of a society, in its political institutions, social structure, leadership, and government activity and policies." (Huntington 1968: 262). It is, as Halliday and Mollyneux maintain, "one of the major social revolutions of the twentieth century". (1981: 12).

The Sudan, on the other hand, experienced its most recent upheavals in 1985 with the ouster of Nimeiri and in 1989 with the overthrowing of Sadiq al-Madhi by a group of military officers. Aside from having a new leader, however, the political and social conditions and structures really changed very little. The traditional leaders regained some power and the system of government and the rough distribution of social and political power remained the same. The coup in 1985, as well as previous ones, changed "only leadership and perhaps policies" (Huntington 1968: 264), of the state without altering either "the structure of political authority or the exercise of economic power" (Trimberger 1978: 6).

The outcomes of change in the governments of Ethiopia and the Sudan are different: one is more revolutionary than the other. In Ethiopia, the class structure and state changed radically. In the Sudan, as with *coups d'état* elsewhere in Sub-Saharan Africa, there was no ensuing revolutionary outcome. In fact, Sudan typifies the pattern prevalent in eight other African states, including Nigeria, the Central African Republic, Burkina Faso, Congo-Brazzaville, Uganda, Benin and Ghana, where coups begat coups. (See Wells 1974; Wells and Pollnac 1988; McGowan and Johnson 1984). The political and social developments in Ethiopia and the Sudan are less known to Western readers than the radical changes in Iran and Nicaragua, for example, but they represent certain types of revolutionary movements that seem to form distinct patterns of revolutionary change in the Third World. They offer a challenge for students of contemporary revolutions in trying to explain these changes.

How can we explain the differences of revolutionary outcomes in Ethiopia and the Sudan? Three specific questions demand explanations: First, how was it possible in both Ethiopia and the Sudan for the military to overthrow the old regime? Second, what explains the ability of the Ethiopian armed forces, in contrast to the Sudanese military, to seize the state power and maintain it? Finally, why wasn't the Sudanese Army able to create a social revolution from above while the Ethiopian army seemed to have succeeded in fomenting a revolution from above? The first question leads us to look for conditions of crucial similarities that made the military revolution possible, including the nature of the state it destroyed or tried to destroy, while the second compels us to specify the conditions of crucial differences. There are similarities between the two countries in terms of both the conditions preceding and the actors participating in the upheaval, yet very different results were reached in terms of both the type of action taken and the outcomes. The last question prompts us to compare and contrast the success and failure of military-led social revolutions. Our analytic strategy is to establish hypothesized causes which the successful revolutions from above have in common and contrast positive cases with negative ones in which the phenomena and causes are both absent, although they are similar to each other in other respects. (See Skocpol and Somers, 1978.)

Trimberger (1978) identifies five salient factors that make "revolution from above" possible. First, the officer class or at least one segment of it should be autonomous or independent of those who control the means of production. Second, the military must develop political cohesion. Third, the military respond to nationalistic or other violent movements and call for political order. Fourth, such military radicals take advantage of favorable international circumstances. Finally, successful revolutions are made possible by the creation of "counter-governments" within the state or in provincial areas. Her emphasis is on structural conditions, not on the actions taken by the military leaders, that facilitate radical changes. There is little discussion of the relationship between the origins of revolution, especially in regard to the nature of the state the military leaders overthrew, and the ability or inability of these elites to promote substantial changes from above. While they conform to many of Trimberger's factors, the Ethiopian and Sudanese cases, as will be shown later, diverge from her given model of revolution.

In the following analysis, we shall compare Ethiopia and Sudan in overall similarities and particular similarities that gave rise to successful military *coups d'état*. We then compare the two cases in the light of crucial differences in their different outcomes of "revolution from above' within state-society relations. We will argue, in addition to Trimberger's specifications, that the different outcomes can largely be explained in terms of: (1) the nature of the state that the military elites destroyed: (2) the strength of state organizations and leadership that the military leadership constructed; and (3) the extensiveness of mobilization and the actions from above taken by the military leaders.

Social Structure and Historical Legacy

The two countries are broadly similar in cultural diversity, social structures and levels of economic development. Sudan is fragmented into 56 ethnic groups and 597 subgroups. The country is basically divided into the majority Arab north and various minority groups in the south such as the Nubian, Dinka and Nuer. Over 115 languages are spoken in the Sudan including 26 major ones. No single language is understood by all Sudanese. Arabic is the language of slightly more than half the population and the official language since 1956, though it is spoken by less than one percent of the southern region. Suni Islam is practised by 70 percent of the population. In the south, Christianity is followed by approximately five percent of the population and the rest adhere mainly to indigenous, animistic beliefs. Sudan is one of the world's 29 least-developed countries ($320 per capita GNP as of 1978) as defined by the United Nations. The agricultural sector employs 78 percent of the labor force. The form and nature of production in rural areas vary in terms of settled cultivation (60 percent of the agricultural sector) versus nomadism (13 percent). Manufacturing growth, estimated at an average 4.1 percent during 1970-1981, is beset with the problems of dearth of manpower, capital, management skills and inadequate communication and transportation facilities. The national literacy rate is 31 percent. Of the population over twenty-five years of age, 91 percent have had no schooling. (Kurian 1987; Niblock 1987).

Ethiopia is an ethnic museum with over 70 ethnic groups distinguished by separate origins, physical appearance, culture, religion and language. The Amharas and closely related Tigrais constitute approximately 35 percent of the population. These two Semite groups occupy the central highland provinces. The Amharas, in particular, regard themselves as founders and historical masters of Ethiopia. Their strong sense of ethnic identity has been reinforced by their role as the upholders and custodians of Orthodox Christianity. Over 70 languages and 200 dialects are spoken in Ethiopia. Among the eight that are spoken by large numbers of people, Amharic is the official language of Ethiopians proper and spoken by at least half of the population. Until 1975 the Ethiopian Orthodox Church was the established church of Ethiopia and was virtually synonymous with the state, and yet only 35 percent of the population and its adherents are spread over ethnic groups and geographical regions. Ethiopia, like Sudan, is one of the 29 least-developed countries of the world $120 GNP per capita as of 1978. It is also a predominantly agrarian society. Agriculture employs 80 percent and manufacturing industry employs 7 percent of the labor force respectively. The national literacy rate is 15 percent. (Kurian 1987; Halliday and Mollyneux 1981).

Sociocultural diversity and underdevelopment, however, do not produce revolutionary movements. On the contrary, they militate against any collective actions and ideologies at the national level as primordial ties and commitment to ethnic kin groups dilute commitment to larger collectivities. Almost every state in Sub-Saharan Africa is multi-ethnic in social composition. In many cases they are arbitrary units in geographical shape and size, population membership, political identity and socio-economic reality. Revolutionary movements in the form of *coups d'état* and "revolutions from above", however, have occurred in some, but not all, of these countries. These social structural features do not distinguish Ethiopia from Sudan in ways which would particularly shed light on the origins and outcomes of revolutionary movements. The crucial cause will have to be found elsewhere, namely, in the historical heritage in general and the feudalism of the centralized state in particular.

According to Skocpol and Trimberger (1978), the social revolutions in France, Russia and China were prepared by the breakdown of old regimes that had been "relatively centralized and partially monarchical states" in predominantly feudal agrarian societies. The main actors and social forces are different but the social revolution in Ethiopia seems to have followed the same pattern.

Prior to the Second World War, the Ethiopian state consisted of the Emperor, the Crown Council drawn from selected members of the nobility and the all-purpose Ministry of the Pen. In the provinces power lay in the hands of a landowning nobility and the smaller landowners beneath them who collected taxes, administered the law and raised military forces when required. The Italian invasion and later competition with Somalia enlarged and centralized the state. Under a new constitution promulgated in 1955, the provincial nobles represented themselves in the National Assembly. The civil service grew from around 35,000 in 1960 to an estimated 100,000 in 1973. This growing apparatus remained under the control of the monarch. The provincial nobility, however, resisted the central authority and maintained feudal control over the land. Thus the monarchy was unable to mobilize the rural surplus for economic growth as Japan did successfully in the 1870s by instituting new systems of taxation and reorganizing land tenure. Rather, as Halliday and Mollyneux observe:

> The resistance of the landed proprietors to reform led to stagnation in rural output, a growing threat of famine, substantial migration of marginalized peasants and a fall in rural taxation. Yet the regime was able to dispense with such reforms and even forgo domestically generated income precisely because they came increasingly to rely on support from abroad. (1981: 20).

Two thirds of the Ethiopian state's capital expenditure, for example, was financed by foreign sources, mostly from the United States, in the last decade of imperial rule. The state became more vulnerable to forces beyond its own control. Urban economy, fiscal accounting, price system, international reserves, domestic currency, inflation, employment, wages, salaries, trade volume and productivity moved in blocks of interdependent correlations. "In 1974 at the center", Halliday and Mollyneux write, "sat a monarchy debilitated in persona and political terms, and increasingly separated both from the traditional aristocracy and new bureaucratic and military elite". (1981: 21) The pre-capitalist state monarchy of Haile Selassie had overrun the normal life-span of its kind and perched precariously at the periphery of a world capitalist system.

The Sudan spent most of its relatively modern history under the joint control of the British and the Egyptians (1899-1956). Prior to this colonial history, the Sudan did not even exist as one political entity: up to 1820-1821, the Sudan was only a collection of regional and local groupings. During the interwar period the southern provinces were treated as a special and separate entity. Tribal and village peoples resisted "alien" central authority, and this reinforced parochialism. When the Sudan gained its independence in 1956, its history was varied enough that no one group had been able to become predominant either socially or economically. The Muslim organizations were divided between the local groupings around a faki and the national organizations such as the Ansar and The Khatmiyyah. The Mirghani family, leaders of the Khatmiyyah, led the opposition to the Mahdiyyah and became allies of the British. Sayyid Abd al-Rahman al-Mahdi (1885-1959), a son of the Mahdi, emerged as the national leader of the Ansar; he succeeded in recreating a national Mahdist organization. Religiously, socially and politically the Sudan remained highly fragmented. (See Voll and Voll 1985: 49-94). The state was unable to centralize its power. The alternation between parliamentary systems and strong leaders that has occurred throughout the Sudan's independent period may have existed because there is a lack of agreement in the country as to what the government of the Sudan should be. This could also, however, be because no government, whatever the type, has been able to integrate diverse social forces into the nation-state.

Ethiopia and the Sudan provide strikingly parallel cases of the way in which external support produced that detachment of the state which was to foster a revolutionary climate. The weakness of Haile Selassie's Ethiopia and Nimeiri's Sudan lay in the overconcentration of power in the hands of a single man. Drought, starvation, inflation, governmental corruption and inattention, strikes and regional conflicts prompted military revolutions in both countries. The major historical variable that facilitated a social revolution in Ethiopia, but which is not a factor in the history of the Sudan, is a centralized state weakened by agrarian feudalism. With the figure of the emperor at the head of the hierarchical class structure, there was a clearer focus of revolutionary hostility. The Ethiopian military was thus able to destroy this dominant feudal class.

The Sudan, however, has long been a factionalized country, with a fragmented power structure. Not only is there geographical fragmentation between the north and south, but there is political, economic, social, religious, tribal and ethnic fragmentation among various groups within the Sudan. The history of colonialism in the Sudan has done nothing to help reduce the factionalism; rather, it has often served to increase it. Since there is this fragmentation of society in the Sudan, it has never been possible for any one group to gain significant control over the entire country. Trimberger's precondition for revolution from above, the destruction of the base of the dominant class, has therefore never been achieved. There is no one dominant class in the Sudan, and therefore no group that the people could unify against. The state was equally underdeveloped and powerless to institutionalize its authority over the entire territory. It was, therefore, easy for any determined military conspirators to overthrow the government but difficult to impose their will upon the society.

Predominance, Autonomy and Cohesiveness of the Military

The military revolutions in Ethiopia and the Sudan were prepared by social discontent and mass actions from below. In the early 1970s illiteracy in Ethiopia remained at 90-95 percent and only eight percent of those eligible attended primary school. "Yet the growth of education to something above zero", Halliday and Mollyneux (1981) observe, "produced a new and influential social category whose very existence challenged the traditional aristocrats and landholders who had till then monopolized the state". (p. 71). "The young and educated people in both civilian and military sector were increasingly aware of the contrast between Ethiopia's condition and that of the rest of of the world". (p. 46). The urban merchants and a small group of businessmen grew restless under the yoke of feudal monarchy. Outside the state apparatus there developed a clamorous coalition of urban opponents intent upon social modernization and greater influence on politics. The blue- and white-collar workers, under the organizational umbrella of the Confederation of Ethiopian Labor Unions (CELU), expressed their discontent. None of these groups, however, was able to organize a concerted drive against the monarchy or possessed a clear idea where the protest should go. The limited size of the urban workforce, together with its dispersal in a wide variety of different sites of employment, failed to develop any sustaining revolutionary workers' movement. In both countries then, the military institution was the only national organization with the necessary resources to contend for power. The army was almost a countergovernment.

The Ethiopian military as an institution came about as a result of the creation of an expanded and partially transformed state in the 1970s and corresponding expansion of education. Haile Selassie drafted the best secondary school graduates into the military academy at Harar. Those coming into the ministries and the armed forces were from a section of the population socially far wider than the traditional nobility. By social origin, most appear to have been children of landowners of at least modest holdings—which allowed some access to education—between the provincial nobility on one side and the mass of *ristegnas* or Oromo tenants on the other. The top officers were mainly Amhara nobility, who came from the elite Harar academy, but the lower ranks of officers and NCOs were drawn from Tigreans, Oromo and Eritereans who graduated from the military academy at Holeta. (Gilkes 1974). The 1974 Ethiopian military revolution can be seen as a conflict between these two army institutions of distinct background and composition, exacerbated by discrimination and differentials in ranks, pay, prestige and power. While no definite conspiratorial group comparable to Egypts's Free Officers can be identified, informal networks, often based on common membership in graduation classes at military academies, certainly existed and began to form a clique which could command politics at the top. The more senior officers drawn from the Harar academy were gradually ousted from the Derg. Equally, however, as the lowest ranks in the PMAC, the NCOs were also generally excluded from the highest positions in the Committee system that evolved. The group that emerged in control was the middle section of the Derg, the Holeta graduates, who had some chances of promotion under the old regime but who were blocked by the nobility and Harar graduates above them. (Halliday and Mollyneux 1981: 141-149).

The longer history of independence in Ethiopia with a longer history of military academy produced a corp of officers in Ethiopia more autonomous and cohesive than that in the Sudan. The Ethiopian military was bigger and more predominant in the state compared to its counterpart in the Sudan. Even before the Ogaden war, Ethiopia maintained the largest armed forces in Africa after Egypt, South Africa and Nigeria. The military expenditure as percentage of GNP was, as of 1959, third in the ranking after Egypt and Libya with 2.2 percent, compared to Sudan's 1.3 percent, and increased to 4.1 percent in 1979-80. (See Halliday and Mollyneux 1981: 148 and Kurian 1987).

The combination of forces that overthrew the Ethiopian monarchy was highly fragmented and factional. Within the military, the power struggle turned violent. The graduates of the Holeta academy eliminated almost all those from the Harar in the July 1976 and February 1977 purges. In the ethnic composition, Amharas are dominant. Although around 40 percent of Ethiopia's population adheres to Islam, only one Derg member is a Muslim. the minority of Oromos, Tigreans and Eritreans have either defected or been executed. Relying often on terror, the PMAC imposed a social revolution from above. It could do so because the military institution was relatively predominant, autonomous and cohesive compared to that of the Sudan.

In the first years of independence for the Sudan, several traditional forces and new social forces stood in conflict against each other: the Ansar and Khatmiyyah, both of Sunni Islam faith, maintained their religious, cultural and social influence. The Sudanese workers, though small in number, were unionized. A most visible change was the increase in the number of Sudanese with modern education who later dominated the political scene, both on the left and right side of the ideological spectrum. None of these political groupings, large or small, however, had the ability to command politics at the national level. Unlike the Shiite hierocracy in Iran, the Sudanese Islamic religious authority provided no national leadership.

In contrast to Ethiopia, the Sudanese military is neither predominant as a distinctive and separate force in the Sudanese political scene nor autonomous and cohesive as an institution. "Instead of being a relatively cohesive interest group", John and Sarah Voll report, "the military tends, in political terms, to be a microcosm of Sudanese society, with all its diversity and its potential unity on specific issues". (1985: 79).

The Sudanese military reflects the history, ethnic diversity and social complexity of the Sudan. Before 1924 all of the 233 Sudanese officers graduated from the Egyptian Military Academy. The Khartoum Military School, established in 1905, produced an average 15-25 officers a year. Most of the cadets who passed through the school came from either Dinka or Nuba origins in the southern provinces. "Military service was only one of a number of paths to a modern-style education or experience and only one of many ways to participate in the modernization of society''. (Voll and Voll 1985: 80). Social heterogeneity, ehtnic discrimination and divided loyalties of the armed forces other than those to the military undermined the institutional identity, corporate interests and organizational strengths of the Armed Forces.

Compared to the size of the country, not only is the Sudanese armed forces small but also less disciplined than the military in Ethiopia. It commands, however, the necessary organizational resources to intervene in politics. The relative frequency of coups and their successes imply that the military within Sudan is something of an independent actor, subject only to the leader of the country when it chooses to be. Nimeiri would have been less likely to have been overthrown had he been a strong and undisputed leader of his armed forces. The military exercises a kind of veto power in cases of political conflict. The July 1976 coup failed largely because the civilian conspirators antagonized the Army. With all the factionalism inherent in the Sudanese political system, the people have been, from time to time, willing to submit to military rule if the military is indeed a fairly nonsectarian institution representing a microcosm of Sudan. During the later part of the Nimeiri period, the army was used both as a kind of business tool as well as political and bureaucratic agent, by the Military Economic Corporation, only to undermine its own morale and authority. (Khalid 1985: 221-226).

Institutionalization of the State

Whether the military bureaucrats can transform social and political structures or not seems to depend on the ability of the state officials, contrary to Trimberger's argument, to mobilize popular forces, rupture with surviving sections of the ruling class and build the necessary organizations to maintain political order and manage the economy. Usually the vicious cycle of coups and counter-coups is a reaction to the "weakness of civilian institutions" (Janowitz 1968; Bienen 1968) and a failure to build "political control structure" (van Doorn 1969: 25-26; Zolberg 1968: 74-79). Coups are also predicated on the failure of incumbent politicians, civilians, or military to arrest inflation and promote a decent level of economic development (McGowan and Johnson 1988; Wells and Pollnac 1988). But above all, the ability to institutionalize the revolutionary state in the broad sense of the term seems to determine whether a military coup can produce a social revolution.

Ethiopia stands in contrast to the Sudan in its relative ability to institutionalize the state: strengthening the army, building the bureaucracy and developing an autonomous state authority independent of class, ethnic and religious forces. Under Haile Selassie, the state power was highly centralized and personalized; neither the bureaucrats nor the military developed corporate interests and identity. The fall of the Emperor meant the collapse of the entire state apparatus. At first, as Halliday and Mollyneux reported, "the conflicts within the PMAC and more generally within the state apparatuses, were both social, between groups reflecting different class interests, and political, between forces advocating different policies with varying degrees of responsiveness to class forces without". (1981: 154) The PMAC's ability to impose centralized control was restricted, given its limited resources and incidences of rural resistance against the land reform measures. The consolidation of the regime in the wake of Somalia's invasion in 1978 involved repression and terror against the revolts in Eritrea and other provinces. The fragmentary nature of Ethiopian society, in which class forces operated in a diffuse manner upon state personnel, and the relative autonomy and cohesiveness of the "Holeta-Amhara" military group that dominated the PMAC and the turmoil of the revolutionary transition combined to provide the state with a considerable autonomy.

The PMAC greatly expanded the military, largely to fight the civil war and defend the revolution, which helped to solidify the military in power. The Ethiopian armed forces grew from 44,000 men and military expenditure around $40 million in 1974 to 75,000 men with military budget totaling $385 million in 1981. Ethiopia's military expenditures in 1983/84 were $504 million, 8.6 percent of the GNP or $13 per capita while that of the Sudan was in 1984/85, $269 million, 1.7 percent of the GNP or $8 per capita. This meant that the Ethiopian military could replace many high-ranking government positions vacated by bureaucrats who fled the country and replace the provincial power-holders with direct military nominees. Over the years since 1976, the state has become more centralized and stronger. By the end of the 1970s, the government erected a system of "professional civil service", state controls and centralized planning. In addition, a new system of mobilization and communication had been established through the political organizations of the regime, such as the Peasant Associations, Trade Unions, Women's Associations and the militia. It was through these organizations that a centralized state was being created. They were not based on recruiting or the operating principles of the old regime; ethnic particularism and heredity played a much smaller part.

Nimeiri fought several opposition groups: he defeated the Ansar rebellion in March 1970 and crushed a communist coup in the summer of 1971. He also faced opposition within the military, some of whom conspired with conservative elements with ties to the old parties while others involved officers who felt that Nimeiri was insufficiently radical. Another perennial source of instability was opposition within the southern region. The Nimeiri government weathered the storms of these oppositions, incorporated more traditional and social forces with the newly-created political institutions and brought an end to the civil war in a negotiated settlement that was finally achieved in March 1972 with the signing of the Addis Ababa Agreement. In 1977 he initiated a formal program of national reconciliation that worked to integrate opposition groups into the political system.

The relative autonomy of the state as it had emerged after the May 1969 coup enabled the regime to implement major reforms. Nimeiri banned all voluntary political organizations and created the Sudan Socialist Union (SSU) as a "forum for political discussions transcending tribal, sectarian, regional and ideological dissension ... and to build in theory and practice ... a new society, populist in origin and revolutionary in organization and practice". (quoted in Khalid 1985: 27). Old traditions of local, native administration were replaced by centralized control. As Niblock observed, however, these institutions "did not encourage that dynamic interaction with population... While claiming to constitute the channels through which the Sudanese population achieved representation, they were in practice subject to regime manipulation and control. Intended to be instruments for change, the institutions were structured such that authority and initiative remained at the center". (1987: 257).

The Nimeiri regime (1969-1985) was stronger and more centralized than the Abboud government that preceded it. Yet it was much weaker than the Mengistu regime in its basic institutional strength from the army and bureaucracy largely because Nimeiri himself failed to institutionalize the power of the state. Instead he personalized it. He not only put himself at the center of the state apparatuses (the bureaucracy, military and Sudan Socialist Union) but Nimeiri made major decisions by himself without consulting the appropriate ministers or directors. He hired and fired his ministers at will and encouraged personalism among his subordinates. Loyalty to him superseded competence in assignment and promotion. Neither autonomy nor professional competence was allowed to develop in these state organizations. The tradition in which a centralized hierarchy of career bureaucrats with expertise who spend their lifetime working on promotion was severely compromised by frequent transfers, whimsical dismissals, poor pay and low morale. (See Khalid 1985: 230-253).

In 1983 Nimeiri, boosted by his third election to the Presidency and also encouraged by promising ties with the Saudis, instituted radical measures to rush toward building an Islamic state. There was the controversial introduction of Shari'a law and the Arabic language to all of the Sudan, undoing the Addis Ababa Agreement by trying to impose "northern" politics and religious tradition forcefully upon the "southern" regions and greater concentration of power in his personal hands. Nimeiri in repeating Abboud's mistake of trying to impose Islam and the Arabic language upon the south had thus dramatically alienated many early supporters and a majority of moderate elements of the society. By the summer of 1984 renewed fighting broke out in the south. Gross budgetary imbalances led to increased deficit financing by the Central Bank. Nimeiri ordered all national banks to abstain from receiving interest, for *riba* (usury) is prohibited by Islam, and introduced a law on *zakat* (religious tithe) abolishing some fifteen taxes. (Khalid 1985: 288-289). Fiscal policies based on radical Islamic tradition and the subsequent repercussions of Shari's law bankrupted the regime. The consequences of all this were soaring inflation rates, huge debt service obligations, unemployment in cities and outcries for political change.

Land Reform and Integrative Policies

The experience of Egypt under Nasser in the 1950s should offer instructive lessons for anyone intending to build a nation-state from above. One of the major and most effective reforms that destroyed the traditional Egyptian bourgoisie was land reform. The compensation value was ten times the rental value of the tenured land, yet the landed bourgeoisie lost their power base to a new constituency under Nasser. (See Abdel-Malek 1968; McDemott 1988). Nasser tried to create a new capitalist class, with limited success, out of the old ruling group and principally from the lower and middle social strata who would support him and give strength and credibility to his revolution. In doing this, Nasser laid the foundation of modern Egypt.

The ''social revolution from above'' succeeded in Ethiopia in part because Mengistu and the PMAC were able to forge a new alliance among newly-mobilized peasants and build a new social basis of political power. Nimeiri failed in his attempt to ''make a revolution from above'' because he was unable to destroy the traditional base of power. His policies were exclusive, divisive and ultimately self-defeating.

Ninety percent of the Ethiopian population live in the countryside. Under Haile Selassie, land ownership was extremely uneven with two percent of the owners owning up to 80 percent of the land. The peasants were subjected to pre-capitalist property relations and to the extraction of rent or tribute from them by a nobility and associated church institutions. Gilkes (1975) and Markakis (1974) estimated that tenancy reached to 65 percent or even 80 percent of the entire households by the 1970s. In 1975 the Derg abolished all forms of land tenture by nationalizing all urban and rural and established a ten hectare (24.7 acre) ceiling on individual holdings. The traditional nobility was destroyed in favor of the tillers of the land. The new military government imposed a radical industrial policy, expropriated enterprises for exclusive state control, renegotiated terms with companies for joint ownership of the means of production and authorized private ownership in certain well-defined fields of activity, such as foreign trade. The Ethiopian revolution offered the population under its immediate jurisdiction the prospect of economic and social development and, after years of turmoil in the provinces, peace and a national identity.

The Derg, however, failed to institutionalize a new relationship between the state and society. Once the radical, educated bourgeoisie realized that its role under the military government was to be little different than its role under imperial rule, much of this class withdrew its support of the new regime. The urban working class, primarily represented in the body of the Confederation of Ethiopian Labor Unions (CELU), also ceased its support of the new government. When much of the urban sector was nationalized, the working class found itself at the mercy of both the Derg and the petty bourgeoisie, who frequently benefitted from the losses of the workers. The peasants, who had initially been supportive of the new regime because of the socialist policies it was espousing, were also beginning to change their minds. ''Like the Russian peasants who claimed they were for the Bolseviks who allocated them land, but against the Communists who forced them to collectivise, so too in Ethiopia'' (Chege 1979: 374). The idea of nationalized land appealed to the rural peasants, but reality found the old landlord class often merely replaced by medium-sized landowners. Little economic improvements in rural areas dampened any earlier enthusiasm for the revolution.

By 1977 the PMAC found itself with very little support outside of some peasants from the southern part of the country. Because of this lack of a broad base of popular support, the regime now had to resort primarily to force in order to stay in power. ''They also made the unpopular move of training and further arming the southern peasants, even going so far as to bring them into Addis Ababa to hunt for underground opposition to the government. Furthermore, these southerners were also used as a militia to fight and try to suppress the perennial uprising in Eritrea, a rebellious northern region of Ethiopia'' (Markakis and Ayele 1986: 189). Neither action served to endear the Derg to the people of Ethiopia.

Despite these early problems in the birth of the Ethiopian revolutionary regime, the government has been successful in remaining in power. Like the experiences in many African countries, the predominance of local and ethnic allegiances proved to be far more powerful than loyalty to the central state. The pre-revolutionary state had rested upon the disunity of the country and on the balance of its various separate components. After the land reforms, however, the revolutionary state based itself upon a new centralized system. In trying to forge a new nation-state, far from making concessions to the various ethnic, class and religious forces, the new government has tried to centralize its power and promote policies that would bring separate components together. There has been no real internal or external threat that has put the power of the PMAC at risk. Instead, the threat brought about, for example, by the invasion of Somalia served as a unifying factor for the people and the government, rather than a divisive factor.

On the thirteenth anniversary of the revolution, September 12, 1987, the People's Democratic Republic of Ethiopia was proclaimed and a new constitution adopted. In addition, a national legislature, the Shengo, was created. Despite these changes, though, Mengistu Haile Mariam is still chief of state and government, commander of the armed forces, and head of the only political party, the Workers' Party of Ethiopia. Thus, in spite of the superficially new look of government, continuity with the revolution is preserved through Mengistu.

When Nimeiri first came to power in 1969 his main opponents were the traditionalist forces in the country, the Ansar and Khatmiyyah, the two major religious sects, as well as the Muslim Brotherhood and their political wing, the Islamic Charter Front. With his ''successes'' in three elections and having ''conquered'' the south with the Addis Ababa Agreement, he now turned against these religious groups. In the words of Khalid:

[T]o strip them of authority and weaken their power base. People, particularly in rural Sudan, [were] still clustering around el Mirghani and el Mahdi (leaders of the Khatmiyyah and Ansar sects respectively). He was more irritated with the latter who was ready to use openly whatever was left of his power base to challenge Nimeiri politically under the guise of religion. So if the only power el Mahdi had was the Imamate, then Nimeiri would metamorphose into an Imam, the one and only Imam of the Sudan. (1985: 256).

Nimeiri polarized politics: at one end of the spectrum there were some groups who stood for Sudanese nationhood and identity, for the unity of the Sudan, for the supremacy of the SSU and the constitution. At the other end stood, for example, the Muslim Brotherhood who wanted to replace Sudanese nationhood even at the cost of alienating the Southerners by insisting on the application of the Islamic legal system to Muslims and non-Muslims alike. In an obvious attempt to impose his will on the South, Nimeiri exploited the divisions and conflicts inside the ranks of the Southerners who soon found themselves spearheading a movement which cut across tribal boundaries. In an ironic twist of events, late in March 1985, Nimeiri suppressed the Muslim Brotherhood, relieving known associates of the Brotherhood from all government posts and arresting the leadership of the organization. Nimeiri thus cut himself off from his last well-organized group of supporters, who now joined the opposition to his radical Islamization campaign. The public hanging of a 76-year old religious figure on charges of apostasy galvanized the public consciousness. Many Sudanese considered the hanging an outrageous violation of Sudan's traditional tolerance. "In the end", as Khalid wrote, "the President not only succeeded in uniting the Sudanese people against him in indignation; sadly, he also made them question the role of Islam in politics. The Islam which the people of Sudan knew and lived under was a religion of tolerance, forgiveness and respect for life and property". (1985: 266).

By 1984-1985 opposition to Nimeiri and his policies was widespread. Violence flared up in the south, and any gains that Nimeiri had previously made there were erased by the September Laws. The economy was also experiencing trouble, and that fact, coupled with the drought, led to increased demonstrations against the Nimeiri regime. Lesch observed that Nimeiri "emasculated the armed forces, cowed the political groups, strangled the business sector, destroyed the independence of the judiciary, and alienated the trade unions". (1985: 2). As Niblock suggests, "a combination of corruption and mismanagement, complemented by the failure to maintain a popular base". (1987: 291) added to the problems of the Nimeiri regime. Given the increasingly worsening situation in the Sudan, it was not surprising that there was yet another *coup d'état* in April 1985.

Conclusion

The analytic approach we have taken highlights the distinction between military revolution and social revolution on the one hand and the structural conditions that led to the successful socialist revolution from above in Ethiopia and the failure of religious-autocratic revolution in the Sudan on the other.

The Ethiopian armed forces successfully seized state power largely because the state was weak and able to conduct successfully a ''revolution from above'' by cultivating a broad social base through land reform. By contrast the military revolutions in the Sudan, especially the recent ambitious efforts by Nimeiri, failed because the military lacked the ability to integrate and institutionalize its power against formidable ''socio-religious'' oppositions. The different outcomes can largely be explained in terms of the nature of the old regime and its relations to the society; extensiveness of the social and ideological mobilization during the revolutionary process; the strength of the organizations and leadership of the military; and the degree of autonomy of the revolutionary elites from the class and ethnic structure. We argue that states vary in history, in their authority relations to society, in the degree of institutionalization of the state and thus differ in their capacity not only to wage a successful *coup d'état* but also to implement successful reforms from the top. In general, however, the more complete the breakdown of the old regime, the more the new military officers are able to build a new state.

Compared to advanced industrial countries, Ethiopia and the Sudan are weak with respect to the institutionalization of state, bureaucratic organizations, formal authority and party system. These features severely limit their capacity to deal effectively with a revolutionary situation whether from below or above. Unlike strong states where leaders can come and go and yet the institutions remain, when a leader leaves the scene, in many cases, the state institution tends to collapse. The state that Mengistu built is far stronger and more centralized than the one he overthrew. Due to the relative autonomy from the class forces and devastating international intervention that he was spared, he could transform the society in a radical way. But the conflict within the state and the inability to secure sufficient cooperation in Ethiopian society has led to a dictatorship, aided by his socialist allies especially the Soviet Union, while in the Sudan in the absence of institutionalization of military-bureaucratic power, a delicate web of interpersonal and tribal agreements and understanding precariously hangs in the balance.

REFERENCES

ABDEL-MALEK, Anouar
    1968   *Egypt: Military Society*. New York: Random House.
AKHAVI, Shahrough
    1980   *Religion and Politics in Contemporary Iran*. Albany: State University of New York Press.
    1983   "Shariati's Social Thought", in *Religion and Politics in Iran*, Edited by Nikki Keddie. New Haven: Yale University Press.
    1985   "Ideology and the Iranian Revolution", in *Iran Since the Revolution*, Edited by Barry M. Rosen. New York: Columbia University Press.
ALGAR, Hamid
    1969   *Religion and State in Iran: 1785-1906*. Berkeley: University of California Press.
    1972   "The Opposition Role of the Ulama in Twentieth Century Iran", in *Scholars, Saints and Sufis*, Edited by Nikki R. Keddie. Berkeley: University of California Press.
ALMOND, Gabriel A.
    1973   "Approaches to Developmental Causation", in *Crisis, Choice and Change*, Edited by G. A. Almond, S. C. Flanagen and R. J. Mundt. Boston: Little, Brown.
    1988   "The Return to the State", *American Political Science Review* 82: 853-874.
ALMOND, Gabriel A. and James S. COLEMAN. eds.
    1960   *The Politics of Developing Areas*. Princeton: Princeton University Press.
ALMOND, Gabriel A. and Sidney VERBA. eds.
    1980   *The Civic Culture Revisited*. Boston: Little, Brown.
ALROY, G. C.
    1973   "The Peasantry in the Cuban Revolution", in *Cuba in Revolution*, Edited by R. E. Bonachea and N. P. Valdés. New York: Anchor Books.
AMARO, N. and C. Messa LAGO
    1971   "Inequality and Classes", in *Revolutionary Change in Cuba*. Pittsburgh: University of Pittsburgh Press.
AMERINGER, Charles, D.
    1974   *The Democratic Left in Exile: The Antidictatorial Struggle in the Caribbean, 1945-1959*. Coral Gables, FL: University of Miami Press.
    1978   *Don Pepe: A Political Biography of Jose Figueres of Costa Rica*. Albuquerque: University of New Mexico Press.
ANDERSON, Benedict
    1983   *Imagined Communities*. London: Verso.
ANGELL, A. and S. Carstairs
    1987   "The Exile Question of Chilean Politics", *Third World Quarterly* 9: 148-167.
ARJOMAND, Said A.
    1984a *The Shadow of God and the Hidden Imam*. Chicago: University of Chicago Press.
    1984b ed. *From Nationalism to Revolutionary Islam*. Albany: State University of New York Press.
    1986   "Iran's Islamic Revolution in Comparative Perspective", *World Politics* 38: 383-414.
    1988   *The Turban for the Crown*. Oxford: Oxford University Press.
ARON, Raymond
    1969   *The Elusive Revolution*. New York: Praeger.
AZAR, Edward E. and Chung-in Moon
    1983   "Islamic Revivalist Movements: Patterns, Causes and Prospects", *Journal of East and West Studies* 21: 79-109.
AZICRI, A. and J. A. MORENO
    1981   "Cultra Politica, Movilizacion Indirecta y modernization. Un analisis contextual de cambio revolucionario en Cuba: 1959-1968", *Revista Mexicana de Sociologia* 43: 1245-1270.
BAECHLER, Jean
    1975   *Revolution*. Oxford: Basil Blackwell.

BAKHASH, Shaul
 1984a *The Reign of the Ayatollahs*. New York: Basic Books.
 1984b "Sermons, Revolutionary Pamphleteering and Mobilization: Iran, 1978", in *From Nationalism to Revolutionary Islam*, Edited by Said Arjomand. Albany: State University of New York Press.
BALOYRA, Enrique A.
 1982 El Salvador in Transition. Chapel Hill: University of North Carolina Press.
THE BANK OF KOREA
 1955 *Annual Economic Review 1955*. Seoul, Korea.
BASHIRIYEH, Hossein
 1984 *The State and Revolution in Iran 1962-1982*. New York: St. Martin's Press.
BAYAT, Mangol
 1985 "Shi'a Islam as a Functioning Ideology in Iran: The Cult of the Hidden Imam, "in *Iran Since the Revolution*, Edited by Barry M. Rosen. New York: Columbia University Press.
BEHNAM, M. Reza
 1986 *Cultural Foundations of Iranian Politics*. Salt Lake City: University of Utah Press.
BELL, Daniel
 1976 *The Cultural Contradictions of Capitalism*. New York: Basic Books.
BENARD, Cheryl and Zalmay KHALIZAD
 1984 *The Government of God: Iran's Islamic Republic*. New York: Columbia University Press.
BENJAMIN, M., J. COLLINS and M. SCOTT
 1984 *No Free Lunch: Food and Revolution in Cuba Today*. San Francisco: Institute for Food and Development Policy.
BIDERMAN, Jaime
 1983 "The Development of Capitalism in Nicaragua: A Political Economic History". *Latin American Perspectives* 10: 7-32.
BIENEN, Henry. ed.
 1968 *The Military Intervenes: Case Studies in Political Development*. New York: Russell Sage Foundation.
BILL, James A.
 1988 *The Eagle and the Lion: The Tragedy of American-Iranian Relations*. New Haven and London: Yale University Press.
BLASSIGNAME, J. W.
 1979 *The Slave Community*, New York: Oxford University Press.
BLACKBOURN, David and Geoff ELEY
 1984 The Peculiarities of German History: Bourgeois Society and Politics in Nineteenth-Century Germany. Oxford: Oxford University Press.
BLAU, Peter M.
 1977 *Inequality and Heterogeneity*. New York: Free Press.
BOIN, J. and Ramia J. SERRULLE
 1981 *El Proceso de Desarrollo del Capitalismo en la Republica Dominicana, 1844-1930*. Santo Domingo: Ediciones Gramil.
BONACHEA, R. E. and N. P. VALDÉS. eds.
 1973 *Cuba in Revolution*. New York: Anchor Books.
BOORSTEIN, E.
 1968 *The Economic Transformation of Cuba*. New York: Monthly Review Press.
BOOTH, John
 1982 *The End of the Beginning: The Nicaraguan Revolution*. Boulder: Westview Press.
BOSCH, Juan
 1964 *Crisis de la Democracia de America en la Republica Dominicana*. Mexico City: Centro de Estudios y Documentacion Sociales.
 1983a *Clases Sociales en la Republic Dominicana*. Santo Domingo: Editora Corripio, C. por A.
 1983b *Composicion Social Dominicana: Historia e Interpretacion*. Santo Domingo: Alfa y Omega.

BREA, Ramoniana
    1983   *Ensayo sobre la formacion del estado capitalista en la republica Dominicana y Haiti*. Santo
            Domingo: Editora Taller.
BRINTON, Crane
    1965   (1938) *The Anatomy of Revolution*. New York: Vintage.
BROWNING, David
    1971   *El Salvador: Landscape and Society*. Oxford: Oxford University Press.
BURNTON, M. G. and J. HIGLEY
    1987   "Elite Settlements". *American Sociological Review* 52: 295-307.
CAMUS, Albert
    1956   *The Rebel*. New York: Knopf.
CARDOSO, Ciro F. S.
    1977   "The Formation of the Coffee Estate in Nineteenth-Century Costa Rica". Pp. 165-
            202 in *Land and Labour in Latin America*, edited by Kenneth Duncan and Ian
            Rutledge. Cambridge: Cambridge University Press.
CASSÁ, R.
    1984   *Modos de Produccion Clases Sociales y Luchas Politicas: Republica Dominicana Siglo XX*.
            Santo Domingo: Punto y Aparte Ediciones. C. por A.
CASTRO, F.
    1976   *First Congress of the Communist Party of Cuba*. Moscow: Progress Publishers.
CESAIRE, Aime
    1972   *Discourse on Colonialism*. New York: Monthly Review Press.
CHEGE, Michael
    1979   "The Revolution Betrayed: Ethiopia, 1974-1979", *Journal of Modern African Studies*
            17: 359-380.
CHILCOTE, R. H. and J. C. EDELSTEIN
    1986   *Latin America: Capitalist and Socialist Perspectives of Development and Underdevelopment*.
            Boulder: Westview Press.
CHILDS, John
    1980   *The Army, James II, and the Glorious Revolution*. New York: St. Martin's Press.
CILLIERS, J. K.
    1985   *Counter-Insurgency in Rhodesia*. Dover, NH: Croom-Helm.
CLAD, J.
    1987a   "The Left's International Lobby", *Far Eastern Economic Review* December 17: 40-2.
    1987b   "The Psinaki's Affair", *Far Eastern Economic Review* August 20: 10-11.
CLARK, Cal and Jonathan LEMCO
    1988   "The Strong State and Development: A Growing List of Caveats", in *State and
            Development*, Edited by Cal Clark and Jonathan Lemco. Leiden: E. J. Brill.
COBB, Richard
    1972   *The Police and the People: French Popular Protest, 1789-1820*. Oxford: Oxford University
            Press.
COBBAN, Alfred
    1964   *The Social Interpretation of the French Revolution*. Cambridge: Cambridge University
            Press.
COPPEDGE, M. J.
    1988   *Strong Parties and Lame Ducks: A Study of the Quality and Stability of Venezuelan Democracy*.
            Ph.D. dissertation. Yale University.
CURRIE, Kate and Larry RAY
    1984   "State and Class in Kenya - Notes on the Cohesion of the Ruling Class", *Journal
            of Modern African Studies* 22: 559-593.
DAVIES, James C.
    1962   "Toward a Theory of Revolution", *American Sociological Review* 27: 5-19.
DEBRAY, Regis
    1968   *Revolution in the Revolution?* Harmondsworth: Pelican Books.
DEERE, Carmen Diane, and Peter MARCHETTI

1981 "The Worker-Peasant Alliance in the First Year of the Nicaraguan Agrarian Reform". *Latin American Perspectives* 8: 40-73.

DELZELL, C. F.
1961 *Mussolini's Enemies*. Princeton: Princeton University Press.

DeNARDO, James
1985 *Powers in Numbers*. Princeton: Princeton University Press.

DEUTSCH, Karl W.
1963 *The Nerves of Government*. New York: Free Press.

DEUTSCHER, Issac
1952 "The French Revolution and the Russian Revolution: Some Suggestive Analogies". *World Politics* 9: 369-381.

DOORN, Jacques van
1968 *Armed Forces and Society*. The Hague: Mouton.

DRAPER, T.
1968 *The Dominican Revolt: A Case Study in American Foreign Policy*. New York: Commentary Report.

D'SOUZA, H.
1987 "Return Ticket to Brazil", *Third World Quaterly* 9: 203-211.

DOUGLAS, Mary and Aron WILDAVSKY
1982 *Risk and Culture*. Berkeley: University of California Press.

DUNKERLY, James
1982 *The Long War: Dictatorship and Revolution in El Salvador*. London: Junction Books.

ECKSTEIN, Harry
1980 "Theoretical Approaches to Explaining Collective Violence", in *The Handbook of Political Violence*, Edited by T. R. Gurr. New York: Free Press.

ECKSTEIN, Susan
1989 "Power and Popular Protest in Latin America", in *Power and Popular Protest*, Edited by Susan Eckstein. Berkeley and Los Angeles: University of California Press.

EDINGER, L. J.
1956 *German Exile Politics: The Social Democratic Executive Committee in the Nazi Era*. Berkeley University of California Press.

ELLUL, Jacques
1971 *Autopsy of Revolution*. New York: Knopf.

ENAYAT, Hamid
1983 "Revolution in Iran 1979: Religion as Political Ideology", in *Revolutionary Theory and Political Reality*, Edited by Noel O'Sullivan. New York: St. Martin's Press.

ENGELS, Frederick
1977 *The Peasant War in Germany*. Moscow: Progress Publishers.

EVANS, P. B., D. RUESCHEMEYER and Theda SKOCPOL. eds.
1985 *Bringing the State Back In*. New York: Cambridge University Press.

FABBRINI, Sergio
1988 "Return to the State: Critiques", *American Political Science Review* 82: 875-901.

FARHI, Farideh
1988 "State Disintegration and Urban-Based Revolutionary Crisis: A Comparative Analysis Iran and Nicaragua", *Comparative Political Studies* 21: 231-256.

FERREE, Myra Marx, and Frederick D. MILLER
1985 "Mobilization and Meaning: Toward an Integration of Social Movements", *Sociological Inquiry* 55: 38-51.

FISCHER, Michael
1980 *Iran: From Religious Dispute to Revolution*. Cambridge: Harvard University Press.

FLOOR, William M.
1980 "The Revolutionary Character of the Iranian Ulama: Wishful Thinking or Reality"? *International Journal of Middle East Studies* 12: 501-524.

FRANCO, F.
1966 *Republica Dominicana: Clases, Crisis y Comandos*. La Habana: Casa de las Americas.

FRANK, Andre Gunder
    1969   Latin America: Underdevelopment or Revolution. New York: Monthly Review.
FRIEDRICH, Carl J. ed.
    1966   *Revolution*. New York: Atherton.
FURET, Francois
    1981   *Interpreting the French Revolution*. Cambridge: Cambridge University Press.
GAMSON, William A.
    1975   *The Strategy of Social Protest*. Homewood, IL: Dorsey Press.
GARVEY, J. I.
    1980   "Repression of Political Emigre - The Underground to International Law: A Proposal for Remedy. *Yale Law Journal* 90: 78-120.
GEERTZ, Clifford
    1973   *The Interpretation of Cultures*. New York; Basic Books.
    1980   *Negara: The Theatre State in Nineteenth Century Bali*. Princeton: Princeton University Press.
GERLACH, Luther P., and Virginia H. HINE
    1970   *People, Power and Change: Social Transformation*. Indianapolis, IN: Bobbs-Merrill.
GESCHWENDER, James A.
    1964   "Social Structure and the Negro Revolt: An Examination of Some Hypotheses", *Social Forces* 43: 248-256.
GILBERT, Dennis
    1985   "The Bourgeoisie". Pp. 163-182 in *Nicaragua: The First Five Years*, Edited by Thomas W. Walker. New York: Praeger.
    1988   *Sandinistas*. Basil Blackwell.
GILKES, Patrick
    1975   *The Dying Lion: Feudalism and Modernization in Ethiopia*. New York; St. Martin's Press.
GILLIN, Donald G.
    1964   "Peasant Nationalism in the History of Chinese Communism", *Journal of Asian Studies* 23: 269-289.
GLEIJESES, P.
    1978   *The Dominican Crisis: The 1965 Constitutionalist Revolt and The American Intervention*. Baltimore: Johns Hopkins University Press.
GOLDSTONE, Jack
    1980   "Theories of Revolution: The Third Generation", *World Politics* 32: 425-453.
GRAHAM-YOOLL, A.
    1987   "The Wild Oats They Sowed: Latin American Exile in Europe", *Third World Quarterly* 9: 246-253.
GRANOVETTER, Mark
    1973   "The Strength of Weak Ties", *American Journal of Sociology* 78: 1360-1380.
    1978   "Threshold Models of Collective Behavior", *American Journal of Sociology* 83: 1420-1443.
GRIFFITHS, A.
    1970   *Black Patriot and Martyr: Toussaint of Haiti*. New York: Julian Messner.
GUERRA, R.
    1974   *En el camino de la independencia.* La Habana: Editorial de Ciencias Sociales.
    1975   *La Expansion Territorial de los Estados Uidos*. La Habana: Editorial de Ciencias Sociales.
GUEVARA, Che
    1968   *Reminiscences of the Cuban Revolutionary War*. Harmondsworth: Pelican Books.
GURR, Ted R.
    1968   "A Causal Model of Civil Strife", *American Political Science Review* 62: 1104-1124.
    1970   *Why Men Rebel*. Princeton: Princeton University Press.
    1972   "The Calculus of Civil Dissent", *Journal of Social Issues* 28: 27-47.

GURR, Ted R. and Raymond DUVALL
    1976   "Introduction to a Formal Theory of Political Conflict", in *The Uses of Controversies
           in Sociology*, Edited by L. A. Coser and O. N. Larsen. New York: Free Press.
HABELSKI, S. and J. KIRK. eds.
    1985   *Cuba: Twenty Five Years of Revolution, 1959-1984*. New York: Praeger Publishers.
HALL, G. M.
    1971   *Social Control in Slave Plantation Societies: A Comparison of St. Dominique and Cuba*.
           Baltimore: Johns Hopkins University Press.
HALLIDAY, Fred
    1979   *Iran: Dictatorship and Development*. New York: Penguin.
    1983   "The Iranian Revolution: Uneven Development and Religious Populism", *Journal
           of International Affairs* 36: 2-12.
HALLIDAY, Fred and Maxine MOLLYNEUX
    1982   *The Ethiopian Revolution*. London: NLB.
HANCOCK, Kelly
    1975   *From Innocence to Boredom: Revolution in the West*. Ph.D. dissertation. Vanderbilt
           University.
HIBBS, Douglas A.
    1973   *Mass Political Violence*. New York: Wiley.
HIRO, Dilip
    1983   *Iran Under the Ayatollahs*. Boston: Routledge and Kegan Paul.
HOBSBAWM, E. J.
    1962   *The Age of Revolution 1789-1848*. New York: Mentor Books.
    1986   "Revolution" in *Revolution in History*, Edited by Roy Porter and Mikulas Teich.
           Cambridge: Cambridge University Press.
HOLLOWAY, John and Sol PICCIOTTO
    1978   *State and Capital*. Leeds: Edward Arnold.
HUNTER, Shireen
    1988   *The Politics of Islamic Revivalism: Diversity and Unity*. Bloomington, IN: Indiana
           University Press.
HUNTINGTON, Samuel P.
    1968   *Political Order in Changing Societies*. New Haven: Yale University Press.
IRFANI, Suroosh
    1983   *Revolutionary Islam in Iran*. London: Zed Books.
JACKSON, Robert H. and Carl G. ROSBERG
    1984   "Popular Legitimacy in African Multi-Ethnic States". *Journal of Modern African
           Studies* 22: 177-198.
JAMES, C. L. R.
    1963   *The Black Jacobins*. New York: Random House.
JANOWITZ, Morris
    1964   *The Military in the Political Development of New Nations*. Chicago: University of Chicago
           Press.
JENKINS, J. Craig
    1983   "Resource Mobilization Theory and the Study of Social Movements". *Annual
           Review of Sociology* 9: 527-553.
JOHNSON, Chalmers A.
    1962   *Peasant Nationalism and Communist Power*. Stanford: Stanford University Press.
    1966   *Revolutionary Change*. Boston: Little, Brown.
    1982   *Revolutionary Change*. 2nd ed. Stanford: Stanford University Press.
KAZEMI, Farhad
    1980   *Poverty and Revolution in Iran*. New York: New York University Press.
KEDIE, Nikki R.
    1966   "Origins of Religious-Radical Alliance", *Past and Present* 34: 70-86.
    1972   "The Roots of Ulama's Power in Modern Iran", in *Scholars, Saints and Sufis*, Edited
           by Nikki R. Keddie. Berkeley: University of California Press.

1980   "Is Shi'ism Revolutionary"? in *The Islamic Revolution in Iran*. Washington, D.C. The Middle East Institute.

1981   *Roots of Revolution: An Interpretive History of Modern Iran*. New Haven: Yale University Press.

1982   "Comments on Skocpol", *Theory and Society* 11: 285-292.

KHALID, Mansour
1985   *Nimeiri and the Revolution of Dis-May*. London: Routledge & Kegan Paul.

KIM, Chong-Yol
1973   "Interviews" by Quee-Young Kim on April 20. Seoul, Korea.

KIM, Quee-Young
1983   *The Fall of Syngman Rhee*. Berkeley: Institute of East Asian Studies. University of California.

KLANDERMANS, Bert
1984   "Mobilization and Participation", *American Sociological Review* 49: 583-600.

KNIGHT, F. W.
1978   *The Caribbean*. New York: Oxford University Press.

KNIGHT, M. N.
1939   *Los Americanos en Santo Domingo*. Santo Domingo: Imprenta Listin Diario.

KOMISAR, L.
1987   *Corazon Aquino: The Story of a Revolution*. New York: George Braziller.

KUHN, Thomas
1962   *The Structure of Scientific Revolutions*. Chicago: University of Chicago Press.

KULA, Marcin
1981   "Los Estratos medios de la societdad en el movimento revolucionario: La revolucion de 1933 en Cuba". *Revista Mexicana de Sociologia* 43: 1229-1245.

KURIAN, George Thomas
1987   *Encyclopedia of the Third World*. 3 vols. New York: Facts on File, Inc.

LAN, David
1985   *Guns and Rain: Guerrillas & Spirit Mediums in Zimbabwe*. Berkeley: University of California Press.

LAITIN, David
1986   *Politics and Religious Change Among the Yoruba*. Chicago: University of Chicago Press.

1988   "Political Culture", *American Political Science Review* 82: 589-593.

LeBON, Gustave
1913   *The Psychology of Revolutions*. New York: Ernest Benn Ltd.

LEE, Hahn-Been
1965   *Korea: Time, Change and Administration*. Honolulu: East-West Center Press.

LEE Ki-Baik
1984   *A New History of Korea*. translated by E. Wagner. Cambridge: Harvard University Press.

LEE Shin-Bom
1987   "South Korea: Dissent from Abroad", *Third World Quarterly* 9: 130-147.

LEE Sung-Chul
1987   "Rebellion Without a Cause: A Stochastic Model of Revolutionary Process", presented at the International Studies Association Midwest, Lawrence, Kansas.

LEFEBVRE, Henri
1969   *The Explosion: Marxism and the French Upheaval*. New York: Monthly Review Press.

LENIN, V. I.
1929   "Where to Begin? in *The Collected Works of Lenin*. Vol. 4, Book 1. New York: International Publishers.

1964   *The Development of Capitalism in Russia*. Moscow: Progress Publishers.

1969   *What is to be Done*. New York: International Publishers.

LEUCHSERING, E. Roig de.
1973   *Historia de la Emmienda Platt*. La Habana: Editorial de Ciencias Sociales.

LESCH, Ann Mosley

136   REFERENCES

1985   "The Fall of Nimeiri", *UFSI* Reports 9: 1-14.
1986   "Party Politics in the Sudan", *UFSI* Reports 9: 1-15.
LEWIS, Bernard.
1988   *The Political Language of Islam*. Chicago: The University of Chicago Press.
LICHBACH, Mark I.
1987   "Deterence or Escalation? The Puzzle of Aggregate Studies of Repression and Dissent", *Journal of Conflict Resolution* 31: 266-297.
LICHBACH, Mark I. and Ted R. GURR
1981   "The Conflict Process: A Formal Model", *Journal of Conflict Resolution* 25: 3-29.
LICHTHEIM, George
1964   "Reflections on Trotsky", *Commentary* 37: 42-54.
LIEBERMAN, Victor
1989   "Vietnamese Communism in Regional Perspective: Metropolitan and Third World Lefts, 1917-1985", Paper delivered at the Third Conference of the University of Michigan Project on International Communism, January 27, 1989.
LIMBERT, John W.
1987   *Iran: At War with History*. Boulder: Westview Press.
LIPSET, Seymour Martin
1972   *Rebellion in the University*. Boston: Little, Brown.
LIU, Michael Tien-Lung
1988   "States and Urban Revolutions: Explaining the Revolutionary Outcomes in Iran and Poland", *Theory and Society* 17: 179-210.
LODGE, T.
1987   "State of Exile: The African National Congress of South Africa, 1976-1986", *Third World Quarterly* 9: 1-27.
LOGAN, R. W.
1968   *Haiti and the Dominican Republic*. New York: Oxford University Press.
LÓPEZ, C. Julio, Orlando Nunez SOTO, Carlos Fernando Chamorro BARRIOS, and Pascual SERRES
1980   *La caida del Somocismo y la lucha Sandinista en Nicaragua* San Jose: Editiorial Universitaria Centroamericana.
LÓPEZ, Segrera F.
1973   *Cuba: Capitalism dependiente y subdesarrollo, 1510-1959*. Mexico City: Editorial Diogenes.
LOZANO, W.
1976   *La Dominacion Imperialista en la Republica Dominicana 1900-1930*. Santo Domingo: Publicaciones de la Universidad Autonoma de Santo Domingo.
MacEWAN, Arthur
1985   "Why is Cuba Different"? Pp. 420-428 in *Cuba: Twenty-Five Years of Revolution, 1959-1984*, Edited by Sandor Halebsky and John M. Kirk. New York: Praeger.
MANGLAPUS, R.
1987   *A Pen for Democracy*. Washington, D.C.: Movement for Free Philippines.
MANIGAT, L. F.
1972   *Evolution et Revolution L'Amerique Latine au XXe Siecle: 1889-1929*. Paris: Editions Richelieu.
MANITZAS, N. R.
1973a   "The Setting of the Cuban Revolution", in *Cuba: The Logic of the Revolution*, Edited by D. Barkan and N. Manitzas. Andovar: Warner Modular Publications.
1973b   "Social Class and the Definition of the Cuban Nation", in *Cuba: The Logic of the Revolution*, Edited by D. Barkan and N. Manitzas. Andovar: Warner Modular Publications.
MARCOS, F. E.
1989   "A Defense of My Tenure", *Orbis* 33: 91-97.
MARKAKIS, John
1974   *Ethiopia: Anatomy of a Traditional Polity*. Oxford: Oxford University Press.
MARKAKIS, John and Nega AYELE
1986   *Class and Revolution in Ethiopia*. Trenton, NJ: The Red Sea Press.

MARTIN, David and Phillis JOHNSON
    1981   *The Struggle for Zimbabwe: The Chimurenga War*, Boston: Faber & Faber.
MARTIN, J. B.
    1966   *Overtaken by Events*. New York: Doubleday.
MARX, Gary T. and James L. WOOD
    1975   "Strands of Theory and Research in Collective Behavior", *Annual Review of Sociology* 1: 363-428.
MARX, Karl
    (1847) 1956   *The Poverty of Philosophy*. New York: International Publishers
    (1848) 1968   *The Communist Manifesto*. New York: International Publishers.
    (1859) 1970   "Preface" to *A Contribution to the Critique of Political Economy*, in Karl Marx and Frederick Engels. *Selected Works*. New York: International Publishers.
MARWELL, Gerald., Pamela E. OLIVER and Ralph PRAHL.
    1988   "Social Networks and Collective Action: A Theory of the Critical Mass III", *American Journal of Sociology* 94: 502-534.
MAZZINI, Giueseppe
    1912   *The Duties of Man and Other Essays*. New York: Dutton.
MENJIVAR, Rafael
    1980   *Acumulacion originaria y desarrollo del capitalismo en El Salvador*. San Jose: Editorial Universitaria Centroamericana.
MERKX, G. W. and N. VALDÉS
    1972   "Revolution, Consciousness and Class", in *Cuba in Revolution*, Edited by R. E. Bonachea and N. P. Valdes. New York: Anchor Books.
MEYER, Jean
    1976   *The Cristero Rebellion: The Mexican People Between Church and State, 1926-1929*. Cambridge: Cambridge University Press.
McADAM, Doug
    1982   *Political Process and the Development of Black Insurgency*. Chicago: University of Chicago Press.
McADAM, Doug., John D. McCARTHY and Mayer N. ZALD
    1988   "Social Movements", in *Handbook of Sociology*, Edited by Neil J. Smelser. Beverly Hills: Sage.
McCARTHY, John
    1987   "Pro-Life and Pro-Choice Mobilization: Infrastructure Deficits and New Technologies", in *Social Movements in an Organizational Society*, Edited by M. N. Zald and J. D. McCarthy. New Brunswick, NJ: Transaction Books.
McCARTHY, John and Mayer N. ZALD
    1973   *The Trend of Social Movements in America*. Morristown, NJ: General Learning Press.
    1977   "Resource Mobilization and Social Movements: A Partial Theory", *American Journal of Sociology* 82: 1212-1239.
McGOWAN, Pat and Thomas H. JOHNSON.
    1984   "African Military Coups d'etat and Underdevelopment: A Quantitative Historical Analysis". *Journal of Modern African Studies* 22: 633-666.
McDEMOTT, Anthony
    1988   *Egypt from Nasser to Mubarak: A Flawed Revolution*. New York: Croom Helm.
MELOTTI, Umberto
    1977   *Marx and the Third World*. Atlantic Highlands, NJ: Humanities Press.
MIGDAL, Joel S.
    1989   *Strong Societies and Weak States*. Princeton: Princeton University Press.
MILLER, John
    1983   *The Glorious Revolution*. New York: Longman.
MOMAYEZI, Nasser
    1986   "The Economic Correlates of Political Violence: The Case of Iran", *The Middle East Journal* 1: 28-40.
MOORE, Barrington, Jr.
    1966   *The Social Origins of Dictatorship and Democracy*. Boston: Beacon.

1978   *Injustice.* Whit Plains, NY: M. E. Sharpe.
MORENO, J. A.
    1970   *Barrios in Arms: Revolution in Santo Domingo.* Pittsburgh: University of Pittsburgh Press.
    1982   "The Dominican Republic Revolution Revisited", in *Contemporary Caribbean: A Sociological Reader.* Maracas: The College Press.
MORLEY, Morris H.
    1987   *Imperial State and Revolution: The United States and Cuba, 1952-1986.* Cambridge: Cambridge University Press.
MOSHIRI, Farrokh
    1985   *The State and Social Revolution in Iran.* New York: Peter Lang.
MULLER, Edward N. and Mitchell A. SELIGSON
    1987   "Inequality and Insurgency", *American Political Science Review* 81: 425-451.
NATIONS, R.
    1982   "Threatened Sanctuary", *Far Eastern Economic Review*, January 22: 18-19.
NEHER, C. D.
    1981   "The Philippines in 1980: The Gathering Storm", *Asian Survey* 21: 261-273.
NIBLOCK, Tim
    1987   *Class and Power in Sudan.* Albany, New York: State University of New York Press.
NOBLE, L.
    1987   "The Philippines: Autonomy for the Muslims", in *Islam in Asia: Religion, Politics and Society.* Edited by John L. Esposito. New York: Oxford University Press.
NUN, J.
    1968   "A Latin American Phenomenon: The Middle Class Military Coup", in *Latin America: Reform or Revolution*, Edited by J. Petras and M. Zeitlin. Greenwich, CT: Fawcett Publications.
OBERSCHALL, Anthony
    1973   *Social Conflict and Social Movements.* Englewood Cliffs, NJ: Prentice-Hall.
    1978   "Theories of Social Conflict", *Annual Review of Sociology* 4: 291-315.
OCAMPO, S.
    1980   "Philippines: The Advantages of Overkill", *Far Eastern Economic Review* November 14: 29-30.
O'CONNOR, James
    1966   "The Organized Working Class in the Cuban Revolution", *Studies of the Left* 6:
    1972   "Cuba: Its Political Economy", in *Cuba in Revolution*, Edited by R. E. Bonachea and N. P. VALDÉS. New York: Anchor Books.
O'DONNEL, G., P. C. SCHMITTER and L. WHITEHEAD, eds.
    1986   *Transitions from Authoritarian Rule: Prospects for Democracy.* Baltimore: Johns Hopkins University Press.
OLSON, Mancur
    1965   *The Logic of Collective Action.* Cambridge: Harvard University Press.
OTT, T. O.
    1973   *The Haitian Revolution.* Knoxville: The University of Tennesse Press.
OVERHOLT, W. H.
    1986   "The Rise and Fall of Ferdinand Marcos", *Asian Survey* 26: 1137-1163.
PAIGE, Jeffery M.
    1975   *Agrarian Revolution: Social Movements and Export Agriculture in the Underdeveloped World.* New York: The Free Press.
    1987   "Coffee and Politics in Central America". Pp.141-190 in *Crises in the Caribbean*, Political Economy of the World-System Annuals, vol. 9, Edited by Richard Tardanico. Newbury Park: Sage.
    1989   "Revolution and the Agrarian Bourgeoisie in Nicaragua". Pp. 99-128 in *Revolution in the World-System*, Political Economy of the World System Annuals, vol. 12, Edited by Terry Boswell. Wesport, Conn.: Greenwood.

PARSA, Misagh
    1986   "Economic Development and Political Transformation", *Theory and Society* 14: 623-676.
PARSONS, Talcott
    1937   *The Structure of Social Action*. New York: Free Press.
    1951   *The Social System*. New York: Free Press.
    1966   *Societies: Evolutionary and Comparative Perspectives*. Englewood Cliffs, NJ: Prentice-Hall.
    1967a   "On the Concept of Political Power", in T. Parsons, *Sociological Theory and Modern Society*. New York: Free Press.
    1967b   "On the Concept of Influence", in T. Parsons, *Sociological Theory and Modern Society*. New York: Free Press.
PÉREZ, L. A.
    1978   *Intervention, Revolution and Politics in Cuba, 1913-1921*. Pittsburgh: University of Pittsburgh Press.
PETRAS, J. F.
    1983   *Class, State and Power in the Third World*. Totowa, NJ: Rowman and Littlefield.
PIERRE, Charles G.
    1981   *El Caribe a la hora de Cuba*. La Habana: Casa de los Americas.
PINARD, Maurice
    1971   *The Rise of a Third Party: A Study in Crisis Politics*. Englewood Cliffs, NJ: Prentice-Hall.
PISCATORI, James P.
    1986   *Islam in a World of Nation States*. New York: Cambridge University Press.
    1988   "Iran and the Islamic Revolution", Lecture given at the Middle East Institute, November 9, 1988.
POOLE, F. and M. VANZI
    1984a   *Revolution in the Philippines: The United States in a Hall of Cracked Mirrors*. New York: McGraw Hill.
    1984b   "Hounding Philippine Exiles: Marco's Secret War in America", *The Nation*. May 12: 577-9.
POPKIN, Samuel
    1979   *The Rational Peasant*. Berkeley: University of California Press.
PRINGLE, R.
    1980   *Indonesia and the Philippines: American Interests in Island Southeast Asia*. New York: Columbia University Press.
PSINAKIS, S.
    1980   *Two Terrorists Meet*. San Francisco: Alchemy Books.
PYE, Lucien W.
    1972   "Culture and Political Science: Problems in the Evaluation of the Concept of Political Culture", *Social Science Quarterly* 53: 285-296.
QUARANTELLI, E. L. and James R. HUNDLEY
    1969   "A Test of Some Propositions About Crowd Formation and Behavior", in *Collected Behavior*, Edited by Robert R. Evans. Chicago: McNally.
RAJAEE, Farhang
    1989   "Iranian Ideology and World View", Paper presented at the Conference on The Iranian Revolution Ten Years Later, School of Advanced International Studies, Johns Hopkins University, February 3.
RAMAZANI, R. K.
    1986   *Revolutionary Iran: Challenge and Response in the Middle East*. Baltimore: Johns Hopkins University Press.
RANGER, Terence
    1985   *Peasant Consciousness and Guerrilla War in Zimbabwe*. Berkeley: University of California Press.

RICHARDSON, John M.
  1987 "Explaining Political Violence: A Dynamic Modelling Approach", in *Countributions of Technology of International Conflict Resolution*, Edited by H. Chestnut and Y. Y. Haines. London: Pergamon Press.
RIVERAND, J. le
  1972 *Historia Economica de Cuba*. Barcelona: Ediciones Ariel.
RÓDRIGUEZ, R. C.
  1965 "The Cuban Revolution and the Peasantry", *World Marxist Review* 8: 12-20.
RÓDRIGUEZ, C. R.
  1961 "El Capital extrajero en America Latina", in *Letra con Filo*, Edited by C. R. Rodriguez. La Habana: Editorial de Ciencias Sociales.
  1983 *Letra con Filo*. La Habana: Editorial de Ciencias Sociales.
ROSEN, Barry M. ed.
  1985 *Iran Since the Revolution*. New York: Columbia University Press.
RULE, James and Charles TILLY
  1972 "1830 and the Unnatural History of Revolution", *Journal of Social Issues* 28: 49-76.
SACERDOTI, G.
  1985 "Keeping the Imbalance", *Far Eastern Economic Review* November 14: 12-13.
SAYLES, Marnie
  1984 "Relative Deprivation and Collective Protest: An Impoverished Theory?" *Sociological Inquiry* 54: 449-465.
SCHWARTZ, B. I.
  1951 *Chinese Communism and the Rise of Mao*. Cambridge: Harvard University Press.
SCHAWARZ, David C.
  1971 "A Theory of Revolutionary Behavior", in *When Men Revolt & Why*. Edited by J. C. Davies. New York: Free Press.
SCOTT, James C.
  1976 *The Moral Economy of the Peasant*. New Haven: Yale University Press.
SEAGRAVE, S.
  1988 *The Marcos Dynasty*. New York: Harper & Row.
SEARS, D. et al.
  1964 *Cuba: The Economic and Social Revolution*. Durham: University of North Carolina Press.
SELDEN, Mark
  1971 *The Yenan Way in Revolutionary China*. Cambridge: Harvard University Press.
SEWELL, William H.
  1985 "Ideologies and Social Revolutions: Reflections on the French Case", *Journal of Modern History* 57: 57-85.
SHAIN, Y.
  1989 *The Frontier of Loyalty: Political Exile in the Age of the Nation-State*. Middletown, CT: Wesleyan University Press.
SICK, Y.
  1985 *All Fall Down*. New York: Random House.
SIMONS, L.
  1987 *Worth Dying For*. New York: William Morrow.
SITHOLE, Masipula
  1980 "Ethnicity & Factionalism in Zimbabwe: Nationalist Politics 1957-79", *Ethnic & Racial Studies* 3: 17-39.
SKOCPOL, Theda
  1979 *States and Social Revolutions*. Cambridge: Cambridge University Press.
  1982 "Rentier State and Shi'a Islam in the Iranian Revolution", *Theory and Society* 11: 265-304.
  1985a "Cultural Idioms and Political Ideologies in the Revolutionary Reconstruction of State Power: A Rejoinder to Sewell", *Journal of Modern History* 57: 86-96.
  1985b "Bringing the State Back In", in *Bringing the State Back In*, Edited by Peter Evans,

Dietrich Rueschmeyer and Theda Skocpol. New York: Cambridge University Press.
1988 "Social Revolutions and Mass Military Mobilization", *World Politics* 40: 147-168.
SKOCPOL, Theda and Margaret SOMERS
1980 "The Uses of Comparative History in Macrosocial Inquiry", *Comparative Studies in Society and History* 22: 174-197.
SKOCPOL, Theda and Ellen Kay TRIMBERGER
1978 "Revolutions and the World-Historical Development of Capitalism", *Berkeley Journal of Sociology* 22: 101-113.
SMELSER, Neil J.
1962 *Theory of Collective Behavior.* New York: Free Press.
SNOW, David A. et al.
1986 "Frame Alignment Processes, Micromobilization and Movement Participation", *American Sociological Review* 51: 464-481.
SOBOUL, Albert
1976 *Problems paysans de la revolution, 1789-1848.* Paris: François Maspero.
STAVENHAGEN, Rudolfo
1968 "Seven Fallacies About Latin America". Pp. 13-31. In *Latin America: Reform or Revolution,* edited by James Petras and Maurice Zeitlin. Greenwich, Conn.: Fawcett.
STEPAN, A.
1980 Papers on Redemocratization. Chp, 2 "Authoritarian Regimes and Democratic Opposition", (Unpublished).
1988 "The Last Days of Pinochet", *The New York Review of Books* 35: 32-35.
STEPHENS, John D.
1989 "Democratic Transition and Breakdown in Western Europe". *American Journal of Sociology* 94: 1019-1077.
STINCHCOMBE, Arthur L.
1965 "Social Structure and Organizations", in *Handbook of Organizations,* Edited by James March. Chicago: Rand McNally.
1982 "The Deeper Structure of Moral Categories", in A. L. Stichcombe, *Stratification and Organization.* Cambridge: Cambridge University Press.
STONE, Samuel
1982 *La Dinastia de los conquistadores.* San Jose: Editorial Universitaria Centroamericana.
SWEEZY, P. and L. HUBERMAN
1960 *Cuba: Anatomy of a Revolution.* New York: Monthly Review Press.
SWIDLER, Ann
1986 "Culture in Action", *American Sociological Review* 51: 273-286.
SZULC, Tad
1965 *Dominican Diary.* New York: Delacorte Press.
1986 *Fidel: A Critical Portrait.* New York: William Morrow.
TARROW, Sidney
1988 "National Politics and Collective Action: Recent Theory and Research in Western Europe and the United States", *American Sociological Review* 53: 421-440.
TASKER, R.
1981 "Interview with Beningno Aquino, Jr." *Far Eastern Economic Review* August 21: 20-2.
TAYLOR, Michael ed.
1988 *Rationality and Revolution.* Cambridge: Cambridge University Press.
TAYLOR, Stan
1984 *Social Science and Revolutions.* New York: St. Martin's Press.
THERBORN, Goran
1977 "The Rule of Capital and the Rise of Democracy". *New Left Review* 103: 3-41.
1980 *The Ideology of Power and the Power of Ideology.* London: New Left Books.

THOMAS, H.
1967   "Middle Class Politics and the Cuban Revolution", in *The Politics of Conformity in Latin America*, Edited by C. Veliz. London: Oxford University Press.
1971   *Cuba: The Pursuit of Freedom*. New York: Harper & Row.
TILLY, Charles
1967   *The Vendee*. New York: Wiley.
1973   "Does Modernization Breed Revolution"? *Comparative Politics* (April): 425-447.
1975   "Western State-Making and Theories of Political Transformation", in *The Formation of National States in Western Europe*. Edited by Charles Tilly. Princeton: Princeton University Press.
1978   *From Mobilization to Revolution*. Reading, MA: Addison-Wesley.
1985   "Models and Realities of Popular Collective Action", Working Paper #10, Center for Studies of Social Change, New School for Social Research.
TOCQUEVILLE, Alexis de
(1856) 1955   *The Old Regime and the French Revolution*. New York: Doubleday Anchor.
TOLCHIN, M.
1986   "High Profile for South Korean 'Embassy in Exile' ", *New York Times* (October 10).
TORRES-RIVAS, Edelberto
1978   *"Elementos para la caracerizacion de la estructura agraria de Costa Rica"*. San Jose: Instituto de Investigaciones Sociales, Universidad de Costa Rica.
TRIMBERGER, Ellen Kay
1978   *Revolution from Above*. New Brunswick, NJ: Transaction Books.
TROTSKY, Leon
(1973) 1942   *Their Morals and Ours*. New York: Pathfinder Press.
TRUMAN, David
1951   *The Governmental Process: Political Interests and Public Opinion*. New York: Knopf.
VALENZUELA, A. and J. S. VALENZUELA eds.
1986   *Military Rule in Chile*. Baltimore: Johns Hopkins University Press.
VILAS, Carlos
1986   *The Sandinista Revolution*. New York: Monthly Review Press.
VOLL, John Obert
1986   "Sudan After Nimeiry", *Current History* 85: 213-216, 231-232.
VOLL, John Obert and Sarah Potts VOLL
1985   *The Sudan*. Boulder: Westview Press.
WALLACE, A. F.
1956   "Revitalization Movements", *American Anthropologist* 58: 264-281.
WALTON, John
1984   *Reluctant Rebels*. New York: Columbia University Press.
WEBER, Max
(1921) 1947   *Theory of Social and Economic Organization*. translated and edited by A. Henderson and T. Parsons. New York: Oxford University Press.
(1921) 1968   *Economy and Society*. 3 vols. Edited by Guether Roth and Claus Wittich. New York: Bedminster
WELLS, Alan
1974   "The Coup d'Etat in Theory and Practice", *American Journal of Sociology* 79: 871-887.
WELLS, Alan and Richard POLLNAC
1988   "The Coup D'Etat in Sub-Saharan Africa", *Journal of Political and Military Sociology* 16: 43-56.
WELSH, Sharon D.
1985   *Communities of Resistance and Solidarity*. New York: Orbis.
WHEELOCK, Jaime
1980   *Imperialismo y dictadura*. Mexico, D.F. Siglo Veintiuno Editores.
WHITE, Alastair
1973   *El Salvador*. New York: Praeger.

WILLIAMS, Eric
  1966   *Capitalism and Slavery*. New York: Capricorn Books.
  1970   *From Columbus to Castrof: the History of the Caribbean*. New York: Harper & Row.
WILLIAMS, William A.
  1966   "The Influence of the United States on the Development of Modern Cuba". Pp.
         187-194 in *Background to Revolution: The Development of Modern Cuba*, Edited by Robert
         F. Smith. New York: Knopf.
WILSON, James Q.
  1973   *Political Organizations*. New York: Basic Books.
WINSON, Anthony Robert
  1981   "Estate Agriculture, Capitalist Development, and the State: The Specificity of Con-
         temporary Costa Rica.: Ph.D. dissertation, University of Toronto.
WOLF, Eric R.
  1969   (1973) *Peasant Wars of the Twentieth Century*. New York: Harper & Row.
  1971   "Introduction", in *National Liberation: Revolution in the Third World*, Edited by Nor-
         man Miller and Roderick Aya. New York: Free Press.
  1982   *Europe and the People Without History*. Berkeley: University of California Press.
WOOD, D.
  1989   "Las Relaciones Revolucionaries de Clase y los Conflictos Politicos en Cuba: 1868-
         1988", *Revista Latino Americana de Sociologia* 1: 40-79.
WOOD, James L.
  1974   *The Sources of American Student Activism*. Lexington, MA: Lexington Books, Heath.
WYDEN, P.
  1979   *Bay of Pigs: The Untold Story*. New York: A Touchstone Book.
YGLESIAS, Martinez R.
  1980   *El Segundo Ensayo de Republica*. La Habana: Editorial de Ciencias Sociales.
YOUNGBLOOD, R. L.
  1983   "Marcos Gets Tough with Domestic Critics", *Asian Survey* 23: 208-216.
ZALD, Mayer N. and Roberta ASH
  1966   "Social Movement Organization: Growth, Decay and Change", *Social Forces* 44:
         327-341.
ZALD, Mayer N. and M. A. BERGER
  1978   "Social Movements in Organizations: Coup d'état, Insurgency and Mass Move-
         ments", *American Journal of Sociology* 83: 823-861.
ZEITLIN, Maurice
  1967   *Revolutionary Politics and the Cuban Working Class*. Princeton: Princeton University
         Press.
  1973   *Revolutionary Politics and the Cuban Working Class*. New York: Harper & Row.
ZEITLIN, Maurice and Richard Earl RATCLIFF
  1988   *Landlords and Capitalists*. Princeton: Princeton University Press.
ZIMMERMANN, Ekkart
  1983   *Political Violence, Crises and Revolutions: Theories and Research*. Cambridge, MA:
         Schenkman.
ZOLBERG, Aristide R.
  1968   "Military Intervention in the New States of Tropical Africa", in *The Military
         Intervenes: Case Studies in Political Development*, Edited by H. Bienen. New York:
         Russell Sage Foundation.

CONTRIBUTORS

FARIDEH FARHI is Assistant Professor of Political Science at the University of Hawaii at Manoa. Her book comparing the Iranian and Nicaraguan revolutions is to be published by the University of Illinois Press. She received her Ph.D. in Political Science from the University of Colorado, Boulder in 1986.

KEITH JAGGERS is a graduate student and research assistant in the Center for Comparative Politics at the University of Colorado, Boulder. Working under the auspices of the Data Development for International Research (DDIR) project, he has been a collaborator on the *Polity II* dataset on political structures and regime change, portions of which are described in a forthcoming article in *Studies in Comparative International Development*.

QUEE-YOUNG KIM is Associate Professor of Sociology at the University of Wyoming. He is author of *The Fall of Syngman Rhee* (University of California, East Asian Studies Monograph, 1983) and co-author of *Education and Development (with Noel McGinn et al*, Harvard University Press, 1981). His primary field of teaching and research is revolutionary movements and social change; and he has published in such journals as *Asian Survey* and *Journal of Developing Societies*. He received his Ph.D. in Sociology and East Asian Studies from Harvard University in 1975.

JENNIFER M. LEACH is in the final year of Master's Program in International Studies at the University of Wyoming. She is currently studying the impact of Catholicism on family planning in rural Guatemala and political roles of women in Eastern Europe.

WILL H. MOORE is a Ph.D. student in the Department of Political Science and research assistant in the Center for Comparative Politics at the University of Colorado, Boulder. He is a co-author (with Ted Robert Gurr & Keith Jaggers) of the codebook for the *Polity II* data set, and a forthcoming article in *Studies in Comparative International Development* which examines the long-run historical changes of the autocratic and democratic characteristics of polities in Europe and Latin America.

JOSE A. MORENO is Professor of Sociology at the University of Pittsburgh. He has published extensively in various social science journals. He is best known for his book, *Barrios in Arms: Revolution in Santo Domingo* (University of Pittsburgh Press, 1970). He received his Ph.D. in sociology from Cornell University in 1967.

JEFFERY M. PAIGE is Professor of Sociology and Research Associate in the Center for Research on Social Organization of the University of Michigan. He is the author of *Agrarian Revolution* and (with Karen Eriksen) *The Politics of Reproductive Ritual*. His critique of Barrington Morre Jr.'s *Social Origins of Dictatorship and Democracy* in its volume is based on an ongoing study of the coffee elites of El Salvador, Costa Rica and Nicaragua. The general theoretical framework for the study is described in his 1987 article "Coffee and Politics in Central America", in Richard Tardanico (ed.) *Crises in the Caribbean Basin.*

YOSSI SHAIN is Lecturer in Political Science at Tel Aviv University, Israel. In 1988-9 he has been a Visiting Assistant Professor at Wesleyan University and Yale University. He is the author of the *Frontier of Loyalty: Political Exiles in the Age of the Nation-State* (Wesleyan University Press, 1989), and editor of *Governments-in-Exile in Contemporary World Politics* (Routledge, forthcoming). He received his Ph.D. in Political Science from Yale University in 1988.

BRIGID A. STARKEY is a Ph.D. candidate in the Department of Government and Politics at the University of Maryland. She is currently working on her dissertation, entitled, "Foreign Policy in Changing Social Environments: The Case of Iran in Comparative Perspective". The primary focus of the work is the dynamic relationship between society and state, and the ramifications of domestic upheaval on the international relations of a state.

MARK THOMPSON is a Ph.D. candidate in Political Science at Yale University. He is now completing his dissertation on the democratic oppositions to Marcos.

INDEX